About
Something
Real

~~~~~~

by
Rob Hill Sr.

Spirit Filled Creations
3509 Kids Court
Chesapeake, Virginia 23323-1262

2nd edition December 2016

Manufactured in the United States

10 9 8 7 6 5 4 3 2 1
ISBN 978-0-9653696-9-5

To my son, Robert Jr., aka, The King.
You're definitely the best thing
I never knew I needed.
Thank you for giving my life purpose.

I love you
- Daddy

Table of Contents

100+

Thoughts For The Day

Acceptance

No matter how long we've known a person, no matter the relationship or bond, you'll only ever know as much about somebody as they want you to know. Just like onions, we all have layers, and we peel them back one by one showing each other new things. Trust people to be whom they've always shown you. That should be the expectation. Anything beyond that should be seen as potential, but not taken for promise. Every adult isn't grown. Age defines time; it doesn't measure maturity. However, we aren't to judge people on the layers they reveal regardless of whether or not we approve. True serenity comes when we trade our expectations for acceptance. To embrace and accept people as who they are does not require you to approve. We all may agree on the necessity of growth and change, but we won't all be in agreement on how we do it.

Just my thoughts, good people. Just my thoughts.

Acceptance & Approval

We all have to live our lives for us. Trying to please everybody is a recipe for the sweetest failure. Be uniquely you and do so without apology. People won't always approve of your choices, like your decisions, or support your dreams. But that doesn't mean you have to change them. The world's greatest frustrations come from people trying to understand things that they weren't meant to. Peace arrives when expectations are traded for acceptance. To embrace and appreciate people "as they are" does not require you to approve of "who they are." You don't always have to like the people you love. Our differences don't define our bonds; they just make our existence distinct. Don't place people in a box, you'll only know as much about somebody as they want you to know. Expect people to be who they've always shown you they are. Anything beyond that should be seen as potential, but not taken for promise. The ability to accept differences and move forward is not only the best quality of successful people, but it's a vital pillar in lasting relationships. Nobody knows your story like you do. People may not know where you came from, but never let them doubt where you're going. Your will to get there matters much more than their approval of your destination.

Just my thoughts, good people. Just my thoughts.

Accountability

In everyone's life, at some point, our inner fire goes out and all we're just blowing smoke. We're talking big, but living small, feeling helpless about this, frustrated about that, and basking in despair. What I don't get is why so many of us complain about always having hard times, but aren't willing to admit that we always pick the hard way. You can't complain about being lost if you've never sought out direction. More often than not, when it comes to hard times, there are many more volunteers than victims. Most of us are hoarders of hardship. We collect and carry our mistakes, pessimism, and dirt around with us giving it opportunity to multiply in our lives. The things happening to us and around us are a direct result of who we are; we've attracted it. Always playing the victim is such an insult to the truth. Hope allows us to bear the rough times today believing tomorrow will be better, but only a fool builds a log house and brings home termites for pets. Times will always be hard, and they'll only get harder, especially if you're not doing anything to make them easier.

Just my thoughts, good people. Just my thoughts.

3

Acting Out Of Spite

What you do when you're angry matters more than what you do when everything's all good. It's easy to do right when you're happy, but can you still do right when everything seems wrong? If you feel like you always have to teach somebody a lesson then you've failed to learn yours. Being spiteful has never done anything to improve a situation. You can live by "Don't get mad, get even" if you want to, but don't get sad when getting even gets you less than you wanted. Adversity tests character, you learn a lot about a man from the things that anger him. Acting in spite does not solve your problems; it only escalates them. Being emotional should not impair your ability to be logical. It's okay to be in tune with your heart, just don't forget to use your brain. Situations that "try you" should not anger you so much that they divide you apart from the real you. Blaming people for your pain does not escape you from the responsibility of looking after your own happiness. Most of the hurt we feel is not caused by the actions of others, but more so by our reactions to their behavior. Abandon retaliation and embrace understanding. Release resentment and welcome forgiveness. Do away with spite and do more with your life. Don't waste your time trying to get even; your focus should be on trying to get ahead.

Just my thoughts, good people. Just my thoughts.

Ain't None Of Your Friends' Business

We all have those people in our corner, those who guide and advise us along the way. They look out for our best interest and love to see us happy. But sometimes those people steer you the safe course and not necessarily the right route. Their intentions are good, they don't want to see you hurt, but what your friends want for you doesn't matter. How you feel and what you want does. So, go for what you want. Saying you're scared to be hurt is subconsciously saying you're afraid of being happy. There is no pleasure without pain. Your friends won't always agree with the decisions you make, for as many times as they're right, the same will go for when they're wrong. When it comes down to it, it's your life. You'll never win the game if you're afraid to take the shot.

Just my thoughts, good people. Just my thoughts.

Anger

Anger is a temporary emotion that denies progress. Don't let your anger consume and control you because that's the quickest route to regret. Expect to be provoked, but be slow to anger. Everything that tries to get your attention should not receive it. The small things making you mad don't deserve the effort and time you're giving them. You're allowing things that are beneath you to feel as if they're equal. Yes, anger is instinctive; however, that anger should never go further than the moment it arrives. The wise aren't absent of anger, they're just patient in their response to it because they understand that whatever angers you, controls you. Patience is the virtue that saves you time, it gives you cushion for mistakes that your anger doesn't always allow. Few things change more often than emotions, but don't allow running with them to set you back. Get rid of those things that incite anger, and those people who encourage revenge. Not holding your tongue may make you feel like you're keeping it real, but it's probably what's keeping you behind.

Just my thoughts, good people. Just my thoughts.

Appreciate Simplicity

When God challenges you, it is to better you not to punish you. When He blesses you, it's not the calm before the storm. It's a gift for your faithfulness. Your tears, your pain, and your struggles are not in vain. God promised you fruits for your labor so when he gives them to you, take the time to enjoy them. Don't be so wired on conquering the next thing that you forget to give thanks and enjoy accomplishing the last. Life moves fast, so fast to the point where we feel compelled to try and keep up, but every race that starts isn't our race to run. Sometimes it's our turn to sit one out and enjoy the break we've been praying to get. Everything in our lives doesn't have to be as hard as we make them out to be. Some people have experienced so much pain that if it doesn't hurt, they can't feel. And that's sad because when God blesses you with a simple situation, the perfect way to thank him is to keep it that way. When he gives you a chance to rest, take it. Don't complicate things with fears from your past or insecurities about your future. Gifts from God come with a lesson, never a curse. Life is an opportunity to benefit from a challenge to be met, and a struggle to accept. Though pain is an effective teacher, it's not the only teacher. Sometimes God would rather teach you through your smiles than to always have to heal you after your tears.

Just my thoughts, good people. Just my thoughts.

Apologies And Forgiveness

Don't be too proud to apologize. The ability to recognize when you're wrong and have the presence of mind to acknowledge it is so pivotal when seeking forgiveness. Apology is an action word; it requires much more doing than talking. You can't say you're sorry if you're not displaying actions of remorse. If you can't admit when you're wrong, don't expect people to acknowledge when you're right. The worst thing you can offer anybody is a halfhearted apology. Don't act like you care if you really don't. A situation may not be that serious to you, but if it's important to somebody you care about, make it important to you. An apology is an act of humility, not a form of degradation, acknowledging that you were wrong shows that you are trying to make it right. We'll all need forgiveness one day. The problem with that is most people want forgiveness from repeat mistakes. However, when you do something over and over again, it gets harder and harder to forgive a "mistake" that you know was really a choice. So, be mindful about your actions. Forgiveness offers a clean slate, but that doesn't guarantee you'll have a new opportunity. You only get but so many chances to mess up before your luck runs out. However, if somebody is humble enough to apologize, be modest enough to accept it. Don't throw away precious time holding onto worthless moments. Nothing wastes more time than an angry mind. What good is it to sit

About Something Real
Rob Hill Sr.

around and be mad in the present about something you can't change from the past? Humility and weakness are not synonymous; sometimes you just have to let certain things go. Not because you're weak, more so because you know it won't matter in the bigger picture. The fact that you've forgiven somebody can never be taken for granted because you didn't forgive for them, you forgave for you.

Just my thoughts, good people. Just my thoughts.

9

Art of Listening

The most effective form of communication is listening. Stop talking, stop thinking, stop analyzing, and start listening. Everybody talks, but few people are actually saying anything worth hearing. Realize that just because you have something to say doesn't mean it needs to be said. What you stand to gain by holding your tongue is more valuable than all you can lose by letting words fly. Most people wouldn't be so frustrated with unanswered questions if they realized the value in observation and listening. The quickest way to get shut out or lied to is to continually interrupt someone every time they try to speak. Just shut up sometimes. Some claim to be listening, but they have selective hearing. They hear what they want to hear, instead of what's actually being said. People are only responsible for what they say and how they say it, not how you receive it. Those who twist words to make them agree with whatever it is they want to hear set themselves up for failure and disappointment. Hearing without actually listening may have you accusing an honest person of lying. So listen to people and don't be so quick to speak. Make sure that what you're hearing is actually what they're saying. So again, just shut up sometimes; you don't always have to agree with what's being said in order to listen.

Just my thoughts, good people. Just my thoughts.

Attract Greatness

Change your thoughts and the way you think because it has a profound influence on the way you live your life. The universe attracts what you put out, so if you want love but think about hurt, you'll get hurt and blame it on love. Your reality is a result of what your thoughts and actions have attracted. Everything and everybody in your life is there because of who you are. If you don't feed yourself the right things, you're only hurting yourself and making room for more of the wrong. Everything is not a coincidence; certain things have to knock you out because pain is the only thing that will wake you up. What has you so scared to the point where you feel you need to act so hard? Put your guard down and pull your faith up. Stop hating the misery of your past and fall in love with the possibilities of your future. Put yourself around people who love, people who are happy, and people who are successful. Watch it manifest in your life. Most get annoyed when you're "in your feelings" because they're scared they may actually have to face theirs. Stop running from you and start living for you. Go through your fears and gain courage from them. Allow your thoughts and actions to work for you and release all doubt because it will only work against you. Feed yourself greatness, and that's exactly what you will put out.

Just my thoughts, good people. Just my thoughts.

Be Fearless. Be Inspired. Be Unstoppable

Don't ever allow anybody to tell you what you can't do. A humble mind has no limits; it only has goals, and nothing will stop it from reaching them. Don't let fear get in your way, don't let opinions deter you, and don't let doubt hold you back. The only thing between you and your dreams is you. How much do you believe in those prayers? How much do you want those tears to stop? How much faith do you really have in yourself? You have to know that all you desire is yours. Not because anybody told you that you couldn't have it, more so because you know you deserve it. Many people fall short because they shoot short. A wise person will always shoot beyond their goals, that way if they fall short, they'll still be in reach of their dreams. Everybody won't be the greatest, everybody won't be president, and everybody won't be the best, but you're not like everybody else. Somebody has to be the leader, somebody has to be the innovator, somebody has to make a way out of no way. Why shouldn't that person be you? When you question whether you're good enough, you put yourself farther and farther away from what you deserve. The question is not if you're good enough; you know you're good enough. The question is if they can handle it. Fear is a common excuse for average people. You can't be scared and be great; they just don't coincide. Be fearless. Be inspired. Be unstoppable.

Just my thoughts, good people. Just my thoughts.

Be You For You

You have to define yourself, for yourself. It's cool to be inspired by somebody, but don't become defined by that person's opinion. Stay true to the things that make you you. Trust yourself; you can't take advice from everybody. The wrong instructions can lead to your destruction. You have to do what works for your life. You and somebody may share the same path, but don't forget you all have different steps. You can copy actions, but you can't replicate favor. Success is reached by dedication, not imitation. There won't always be somebody there to lean on, so learn to depend on you. Trust people to be there, but don't need people to be there. Some of the toughest battles you'll face in life will be with yourself. Trust, love, and believe in you enough to handle them. You want support? Support yourself. You want respect? Respect yourself. You want love? Love yourself. It starts and ends with you. You can't allow certain things or people to hold you down. Anything that can't promote you will eventually contribute to demoting you. People will want you happy; people will want you successful. People will want you here; people will want you there. But what people want for you means nothing if it's not what you want for yourself. Trying to be what everybody else wants you to be is the fast track to misery. Be you for you.

Just my thoughts, good people. Just my thoughts

Beautiful Surprises

Don't you think it's better to be extremely happy for a short while, even if you lose it, than to just be okay your whole life? It baffles me how so many choose to just be "okay" or "content" their whole life. Shortcomings lead them to stop dreaming and goal setting, and it's not always guaranteed that you will lose the happiness. But the fear that losing it is even possible has too many people scared to do what it takes to get it. I refuse to be bullied by pain, intimidated by hurt, or frightened by the possibilities of disappointment. So what if I shoot for the moon and miss a thousand times. I'll keep shooting, and if I never make it at least I'll know what being with the stars felt like. We go through all the monotonous moments life gives us for that one shot at spontaneity, that one chance to land on cloud nine, and that one moment we could live in forever. We don't live life for its dependable let downs; we live life for the few times where words won't do its beautiful surprises' justice.

Just my thoughts, good people. Just my thoughts.

Because I Was Mad

I wonder if the things people say when they're mad are really the way that they feel or if they just wait until they're mad to have the guts to say it? I wonder if they know that when words are spoken in anger, they leave scars. The verbal wound is just as bad as the physical one. In most cases it's actually worse because words don't die. Sure we can brush some things off, but when it hurts, no matter what we do, the words seem to echo, and the feeling always seems to linger. It's like you can put a knife in a person and take it out. But it won't matter how many times you say I'm sorry, the wound will still be there. Our hearts may forgive, but our minds never forget. It's only so many times, 'I was mad,' should be used as a person's excuse not to control their temper. Anger is an internal force; it starts within and ends within. Sometimes it's as elementary as counting to ten. Think first.

Just my thoughts, good people. Just my thoughts.

15

Believe In Change

I know about liars because I've been one. I know about games because I've played them. I know about mistakes because I've made plenty. But I also know about change because I've done that. Stop thinking that people never change. They may not do it on our time or as fast as they should, but give hope to those who don't stop trying. Uplift people; remind them of what the future says they can be instead of what the past says they used to be. Slow change is far greater than no change. Trying to do better isn't always easy, but support and prayers go a lot further than judgments and criticism. If you know somebody trying to change for the better, support them before you doubt them. People do change, they just don't change overnight, and if they do, don't trust it because real change is gradual. If you have dreams of being a better you, keep away from people who try to belittle your ambitions. It's never too late to try and do better because when you're through changing, you're through living. Everybody has a past; you don't have to hide in it, if you're brave enough to rise from it. Anybody with the will to change, can change. It starts and ends with you.

Just my thoughts, good people. Just my thoughts.

Both Sides Of The Fence

Some say if you want certain things, you have to be patient and let them come to you. They say things like you can't rush it or you just have to let things happen naturally, and I'm not sure if I completely agree. If you really care about something, and you want it that bad, shouldn't you go get it? I think one major flaw; we all lack is discretion in decision-making. We confuse waiting on the things we can't control with doing what it takes to go get the things we can. Certain things are in our scope, they're in our grasp, and they're waiting for us to take that leap of faith and do what it takes to get them. They won't just fall in our lap; they won't chase after us; they won't force us to receive them even though they're meant for us. Opportunities and moments are meant to be seized, not left to sit idle waiting on us to build up some false courage. Now more than ever, we need to be the type of people that make things happen. We need to make decisions on those doors we leave cracked because we don't know whether we should close them or walk through. At the end of the day, it's the difference between us actually wanting all we say we want, or us just liking the way the thought of it sounds.

Just my thoughts, good people. Just my thoughts.

Can You Handle The Truth?

Sometimes the truth alone isn't enough. Most people won't accept the pure truth until it's stained with some dirty actions. It's like people don't recognize the end unless it comes with a tragedy. It shouldn't take for your hand to get cut off for you to know when to let go. It shouldn't always take a broken heart for you to see that you're investing feelings into the wrong person. Wake up. So many people are frustrated asking for truth, but they aren't recognizing when they've been getting it. When you can't handle the truth, you usually end up lying to yourself before you get the chance to be lied to. Learn when enough is enough. If you feel the heat from the fire, why touch it and complain when you get burned? 90% of behavior is habitual. So, if you aren't happy with the way things go in your relationship life, change your dating habits. If every break up is the same for you, then you may need to break it down and be single for a while. Learn some things about yourself and reassess what it is you think you like. You can't be superman but be attracted to kryptonite. Watch what you wish for. If you're the girl who loves bad guys because the good ones are boring, then heartbreak must excite you. Stop lying to yourself saying that you want to change, but you're still doing the exact same things that you did yesterday. You can't help whom you love, but you can help who you allow to hurt you. You don't always have to hear the truth to know the truth, but once you know it, be prepared to handle it.

Just my thoughts, good people. Just my thoughts.

Can't Measure Your Weight On Someone Else's Scale

Who you are. What you do. Why you like the things you like. Your goals. Your dreams. Your ambitions. They are all what makes you YOU. They shouldn't be dependent upon what those in your family have always done. They shouldn't be reliant upon the direction your friends have decided to take. Doesn't matter what faults others deem you to have. Doesn't matter how much baggage people complain about you carrying. Your weight is measured on your scale. Your shortcomings are birthed through yourself evaluation along with the wisdom God has given you to detect them. Where your friends are in life has no relevance on your position and where you plan to go in yours. Make your own trail, at your pace, doing what's right for your life. While others may hold insight and opinion on the things you do, what matters more than anything is the vision, direction, and sense of purpose God has for your life.

Just my thoughts, good people. Just my thoughts.

Certain Wounds Only Heal Over Time

Life can cut you deep; it's truly an emotional roller coaster. Lovers become resentful, best friends become strangers, and dreams dry up like raisins in the sun. Sometimes, you can't help it, other times you can, and then there are those rare times when you can, but you just don't want to. Most things just take time. Regardless of what you do, nothing lasts forever. Things rarely go back to what they "used" to be, and realistically, they aren't supposed to. It's the natural evolution of growth. There are reasons for every season so value the lesson and respect its purpose. Time is the most effective healer, so just breathe maybe give time...time.

Just my thoughts, good people. Just my thoughts.

Challenges Of Boredom

If you're always bored, it's not because there's nothing to do, it's because you choose to do nothing. People who claim boredom are those who refuse to consistently challenge themselves. Subconsciously they're bored because they're waiting on something, but anxious to do nothing. You'll never hear successful people talk about being bored; success is a state of mind, and boredom is a state of pity. Most times it's not the things you are or aren't doing that bore you, it's yourself. If you ever have the opportunity to reach for more but settle for less, you'll always get less than you settled for. Don't struggle between what you have to do and what you want to do because successful people don't have time to complain about either. Having a comfort zone may keep you content, but that contentment will suppress your joy. Boredom is an expression of a closed mind and a direct representation of a limited individual. Lucky people are bored and have time to wait for things to happen. Blessed people are divinely advised to make things happen. Remember this: the word can't create obstacles while the word can create opportunity. Challenge yourself to get up, get active, and put boredom behind you.

Just my thoughts, good people. Just my thoughts.

Changing You to Better You

If you have people in your life that push you, pray for you, and encourage you, then embrace that. They see the best in you. The people who only recognize your good qualities are the worst for you. They should see the beauty in your flaws just as they do your strengths. If you find somebody always willing to bring you up in the midst of your downs, you've found a winner. Some people are genuinely giving you time and effort because they believe in you, not because they want to change you into somebody else. Learn to receive certain things with a mature mindset. Don't allow your pride to have you thinking with a closed mind. Never be above change because that puts you below growth. You can't be naïve; we all have areas of life that we can improve in. You have to know the difference between somebody trying to change you and somebody wanting to better you. If you find somebody that's willing to fight for you, you're a fool if you choose to give up on them. Being good is okay, but it's only useful when you decide to do good as well. Nobody reaches greatness on their own. You can learn something from everybody. Get right when you know right. Don't always wait until things go wrong, you may end up losing something you can't get back. If you can do a little, then do a little. Something is always better than nothing. Minor change can influence major progress.

Just my thoughts, good people. Just my thoughts.

Choices

The beautiful thing about life is that we have the opportunity to choose. We choose when to give up; we choose when to give in, and when to give it our all. The choices we make mistakenly are just as important as the decisions we come to deliberately. You get a thousand choices a day and each one counts. Choose who you'll be in life, choose what you'll stress, and choose what matters to you. Don't ever let anybody tell you that you can't be great. Know who you are, know what you do, and know what's real to you. Nothing else matters after that. Don't waste time trying to prove how different you are to people whom only want to see you for who you used to be. You don't need people to believe that you can change in order for you to change. Honestly, if you clear some of the pessimistic stress causing people from your life, you might be able to make room for some joy. It's hard to have a parade around people constantly praying for rain. Changing your circle can really change your life. Choose carefully whom you allow to get close to you. Understand that the choices you make in your life are for you. It's neither realistic nor necessary to expect everyone to agree with them. Nothing is going to happen for you unless you decide that you're going to make it happen for yourself. No failure or fear should keep you from fighting for your future. If you're too focused on where you've been, you'll never see where God is trying to take you. Life is all about choices. Make sure you choose wisely.

Just my thoughts, good people. Just my thoughts.

Comfort Of Control

I need a change. I need some excitement. I need to wake up in the morning smiling about the possibilities of my day. I need something new. I need a spark. I need the butterflies' new beginnings and welcomed challenges incite. I need the things I want to be seen as needs because the facts are, I don't know what I need. I just base the things I think I need off the constant changes of my wants. In reality, what I really need is a new mindset, a refreshed spirit, and a sweet slow dance with humility. I need to take today and make it the best reality it can possibly be in hopes that God will see how grateful I am and graciously bless me with what He knows I need. I've been making decisions based off what I thought I needed for too long and it just doesn't produce the results I "need" it too. So, today my prayers change from what I think I know to trusting what He knows. Believing that what God has for me is much more than what I had for myself. My suggestion is you do the same.

Just my thoughts, good people. Just my thoughts.

Comfort Zone

Start thinking with an open mind. You can't be afraid to step outside of your comfort zone. Of course, you have your preferences, the things you like, and what you think you want. But what if what you want is blocking you from what you need? What if what you like is keeping you from something you could love? What if what you prefer is stopping you from receiving what you deserve? You can't continue living life just going with what you're used to. There's no progress in that. They say if it's not broke don't fix it, but just because it isn't broke doesn't mean it can't get better. Show me something that can't improve, and I'll show you a something you no longer need. Switch it up sometimes. Trying new ways opens up the door to new possibilities. Most people can't get ahead in life because they're too comfortable with where they are. The first step to becoming great is realizing that good just isn't enough. Don't allow fear to stunt your growth. You can't rise up if you're scared to be let down. If you want to be the best, you can't avoid the work, and you can't be scared of the process. The top isn't for you if you're scared to fall. Take a chance on something. The worst that can happen is that you learn something new. Search for the truth in all you do, find what's real, and stay true to that. Nothing gives unless you give first. Nothing changes unless you change first.

Just my thoughts, good people. Just my thoughts.

Communication

Communication is such a big deal when it comes to easing frustrations. Sometimes we wait until things are a little too late to discuss what needs to be said. If you care enough to be angered or saddened by a situation, then you should care enough to talk it out. It's not about always being the bigger person. It's about recognizing an issue, caring enough to confront it, and moving on. Silence welcomes assumptions; communication kills them. Don't use the "I don't want to argue excuse" because enemies argue; friends discuss. In relationships, the ability to talk things out is foundational, not always to explain yourself, but more so for understanding. No relationship is perfect, but if the good times outweigh the bad times, I suggest you work it out because it's all worth it. Some things will be hard to say, but that doesn't mean they shouldn't be said. If you're ever trying to find the best way to say something, just speak it from your heart. Genuine words don't have to flow like rivers in order to move mountains. Never be afraid to speak what's on your mind, but make sure it's done in a way that you would want to be spoken to.

Just my thoughts, good people. Just my thoughts.

Compromise, Forgiveness, Progress

You have to move on from certain situations. Don't claim you've forgiven somebody, but bring up the past every time you get angry. There is no progress in the past. That's why you can't go back to it. Learn how to look forward. There's nothing wrong with arguing, but it's pointless if you keep having the same ones.   In relationships, you won't always agree. Figure out a way to compromise so you can get past the argument and get to the solution. Learn to meet your partner halfway; it's better to bend a little than to break. If you're not willing to compromise, then be prepared for complications. You can't always get your way when you want it. Sometimes the personal battles have to lose, in order for the relationship to win. An apology isn't saying one is right and the other is wrong; it's just a sign that happiness is more important than pride in the relationship. If you make an agreement, stick to it. Plans shouldn't change just because your emotions have. Be honest about what you want. Consenting to something you disagree with just to avoid a problem only ends up creating more issues. Seeing eye to eye is impossible if you're thinking with a closed mind.

Just my thoughts, good people. Just my thoughts.

Confidence

You shouldn't always need a compliment to have confidence. Self-worth should never be determined or validated by others. What people say about you is what people say about you. Don't stress the things you can't control. There's no point in addressing everybody coming at you. Some people only speak on you to get attention from you. Secure people are comfortable being hated for who they are; the insecure seek love trying to be something they're not. If the "real you" is ever questioned, the people who matter will know the truth, and the ones who don't won't believe you anyway. It's foolish to seek approval in things/people that have no authority. Understand that every person passing judgment isn't a judge. How you portray yourself is the way people will perceive you, and the way you treat yourself is how people will treat you. Self-respect is the only respect that matters. When you respect yourself, your presence alone commands it from others. Fight to maintain your character, not your reputation. Character is who you really are; reputation is merely what others think of you. Sometimes you'll find yourself feeling like it's you against the world, and in those times, you need to know how to encourage yourself. A compliment should confirm what you already know, not define who you are. There won't always be somebody there telling you you're beautiful, or telling you you're smart, or praising your talents. If you don't know how to build yourself up, you'll fall for anybody trying to break you down. Learn how to encourage yourself.

Just my thoughts, good people. Just my thoughts.

Confusions, Insecurities, Concerns

Whether we know it or not, we all have similar issues. We share confusions, we share insecurities, and we share concerns. When it comes to relationships, most of our confusion comes from insecurities that we try to hide as concerns. The difference between them comes in the timing of the two. Concerns can be spoken in confidence; insecurities come in moments of vulnerability. Insecurity is an internal disease, your partner's actions may comfort them, but only you can cure them. The wise recognize that confronting insecurities is the first step to security. Having a weakness doesn't make you weak, just as having an insecurity doesn't make you insecure. Addressing both can only improve you. Most people would rather have the courage to reveal their insecurities than deal with the confusion of trying to hide them. The worst way to solve a problem is to act as if there isn't one. I'd rather look soft and be solid than to appear whole and be broken. When you have a good partner, an addressed insecurity usually turns into a confident concern. So solve situations when you can and stop letting your confusion ruin good things. Insecurities end friendships; concerns improve them.

Just my thoughts, good people. Just my thoughts.

Convenient Love

If you're looking for a convenient love, it doesn't exist. Real love comes with terms and conditions that you're going to have to uphold. It's going to ask you to step out of your comfort zone, to sacrifice, and to compromise. If you can't agree to those, love won't agree with you. Ask yourself what it is you really want; do you want convenience or happiness? A hurt woman will recognize a good man, but won't know how to accept him if she's allowed her pain to divide her. A scared man will easily miss a good woman because he knows what to run from, not what to look for. We all have this warped perception of whom we're supposed to be with. We try to find our partners based off of our past mistakes instead of God's direction, and that's why we're lost. Don't ever confuse being different with being better. Every person you have a connection with won't be the person you're supposed to have a relationship with. Everybody isn't meant to last a full season in your life. Some people are just that one day of 60 degree weather in the winter cold. Don't be fooled into thinking you can make love appear and disappear when it benefits you. Love doesn't happen on your time, it happens at the right time. And only God determines that.

Just my thoughts, good people. Just my thoughts.

Day By Day

Take things one day at a time. You can't keep beating yourself up about your past; it will only make you too worn out to handle the present. Stop wrestling with the doubts, let go of the guilt, and let go of the regrets. What happened, happened, let it go and pay attention to what's happening. Accept your flaws, acknowledge your strengths, and let them work together in making you the best person you can be today. Make a plan, set a goal, and see it through with determination and focus. What you put on the back burner may come back to burn you. Don't procrastinate. There's virtue in patience, not in waiting. Learn the difference between when it's not your time and when you're wasting time. You can't get uneasy, don't move in haste, because that will lead to avoidable mistakes. Think things through and have faith in your ability to make the right choice. You can't be so focused on making the wrong decision that you overlook making the right one. Every mistake isn't a foolish one. Sometimes it will take a mistake to show you your misstep, so let experience teach you. Don't get down just because you don't know. When it looks like nothing is changing, you're looking at the wrong things. Things are always changing; make sure your attitude allows you to see them.

Just my thoughts, good people. Just my thoughts.

31

Dealing With Things

There's a difference between moving on and giving up. It's not giving up if your partner was too proud to ever give in. When it's over, let it be over. Be courageous in your fights and battles, but be wise enough to recognize when you're fighting the wrong fight. You can't "work it out" if your partner is not willing to work with you. Nobody wants to be the one who gave up, but why are you refusing to quit a war you were never called to fight? Some people have broken certain parts of themselves that only they can fix. You can't expect to get love back from somebody who never wanted to receive it. When you find yourself ignoring the issues that bother you just to "keep the peace", you're officially killing your relationship. Communication is the heart of any bond. When it stops working, things start ending. Anybody can run from their problems, but no matter how far they run, they have to take their heart with them. So, stop trying to avoid issues and learn to confront them so you can get your healing. If you have to go outside of your relationship to find a smile, something needs to change. If you have to leave your home to find peace, something needs to change. And when you're honest enough with yourself to see that things need changing, do what you have to do to change them. Moving on isn't giving up, avoiding problems doesn't solve them, and every battle isn't yours to fight. Once you learn this, unnecessary stress will leave you.

Just my thoughts, good people. Just my thoughts.

Denial

Doubts and denials are the sponsors of wasted time. The "if's" that they provide often give people more regrets than plans. Sometimes the "could haves" are hard to accept, but understand that the "could" in that phrase implies that it wasn't for you. What is supposed to happen, always happens, it just doesn't always happen in ways that we like. When life hits you, there are only two options – Accept and change or deny and suffer. When you choose the route of denial, just know you've chosen a path full of delays. You can't fear the truth; the harshest lies you'll ever experience will be the ones you tell yourself. If it hurts, don't tell yourself it doesn't. If you care, don't try to hide that you do. Healing comes through recognition. Fronting will always put you behind. When it comes to love the worst thing you can do is deny it. When you find that special someone, don't let anyone or anything get in your way. In certain situations, you only get one chance to do it right, so take your time. Impatience makes you sloppy. Thinking things are possible leaves them to chance, but knowing things are possible gives you the power to make a choice. Choose to face those things about your life that aren't so easy to accept; the moment you do this you're ready to change them. There is no peace in denial, only in truth. You can't run from what you know. Use it all to your advantage.

Just my thoughts, good people. Just my thoughts.

Determination > Doubt

No matter what you attempt to do, there will always be somebody who will feel the need to tell you that you can't. There will always be haters, there will always be doubters, and there will always be non-believers. And then there will always be you, proving them wrong. If hearing the hate is the only thing that motivates you, then you'll always be a step behind. You're wasting valuable time if you wait for somebody to say you can't just for you to realize that you can. True motivation should come from knowing what you deserve, not from people telling you what you can't have. You can't be scared to try a little longer, to love a little harder, and to give a little more. The extent of your rewards in life will always be connected to the measure of your risk. If you want it all, be prepared to give it all. Don't allow the occurrences of another person's life to block the experiences of yours. Find out for yourself. You can't always go off of what people tell you. Learn to be exactly what you are and confidently let the world know who that is. Be you without apology because at the end of the day, it's not about what people call you. It's about what you answer to. It's not about what people blame on you; it's about what you accept responsibility for. It's not who people say you aren't, it's about who you know you are. When you accept somebody else's definition of you, it steals your ability to define yourself. Know who you are, know what you can do, and never waiver in that. In the end, nobody remembers who doubted your life, they only remember what you did with it.

Just my thoughts, good people. Just my thoughts.

Disappointment

Your level of disappointment is determined by your measure of expectation. It doesn't mean expect less; it just means that you just have to be able to handle more. Stop lowering your expectations, and start increasing your strength. When you expect nothing, you get nothing. Disappointment, failure, and pain build things within you like character, humility, and patience. You don't get the diamond without the pressure. Love is never truly lost when wisdom is gained. You'll lose a few relationships when God's trying to give you a marriage. Sometimes a loss in the present is the perfect set up for a win in your future. Don't shut people out every time things go wrong. You could be sealing off healing and hope. Just because a few people let you down, it doesn't mean everybody wants to do the same. Some genuinely want to help you. It'll be hard for you to recognize God sending you an angel if you have your mind made up that everybody is the devil. Today's situation isn't the end of your story, stop letting bad things block you from turning to the good pages. Disappointment only occurs for a moment of time, not for the rest of time. Learn how to get over things in a way that makes you better, not bitter.

Just my thoughts, good people. Just my thoughts.

Do Half Of Nothing

If you're going to start something, see it through to the finish - that's the essence of success. At times, our mistakes can block us, our failures blind us, and our shortcomings bind us. We put ourselves in this self-confined prison with our thoughts and beat ourselves down over and over again. We think of all the times where we could have done one thing and chose to do another. In life, we all get knocked down, we all fail, and we all lose. But what happens to you doesn't matter half as much as what you decide to do about it. You won't always feel happy, you won't always feel attractive, and you won't always feel successful. But everything you feel isn't always real. Don't be ruled by your emotions, be the ruler of your thoughts. Life is not about how fast you run the race; it's about having the courage not to stop. Speak this when you find yourself looking back and somehow expecting to go forward: There is no potential in my past, only the promises of my future.

Just my thoughts, good people. Just my thoughts.

Do Right

Most people know what's right, but they ignore what's right when it comes to what's convenient. Don't wonder why you always come up short when all you take is shortcuts. Some people are gluttons for pain and hoarders for hardship because that's all they understand. They'd rather be hurt than happy because there are no surprises in misery. Bad times are hard to forget, but the good times are even harder to remember because there is no scar for happiness. We remember pain, but we dismiss joy. Why nurse your bruises but neglect your blessings? Faith beats bad luck any day because in faith, luck does not exist. The truth is harder to accept than it is to find, so don't have your vision so focused on the rain that you forget to enjoy the rainbow. Sometimes you'll fall short, but don't live in regrets. Refuse to resort back to your old ways. If they were working, you wouldn't have changed them. It doesn't matter how slow you walk, just be wise enough to never walk backwards. Learn from experiences, if you don't get back when God warns you, you'll get pushed back when life hits you. When you know right, do right, regardless of what's convenient or easy.

Just my thoughts, good people. Just my thoughts.

Does 2 + 2 Still Equal 4?

Isn't the whole dating process ironic? We go through all these pointless motions. We set all these rules, standards, and expectations for our perspective partners. And the one that we actually choose ends up being the ones we make all the exceptions for. We say we want romance, we say we want true love, but all we really want is a checklist. Are they perfect? Are they attractive? What car do they drive? Where do they work? What school did they attend? What Greek organization did they join? For the rare few who fit the criteria, don't play yourselves because people don't actually fall in love with people anymore, they fall in love with how close you meet the points on their calculated checklist. Money over substance; looks over soul; polished over principles. Doesn't matter how real or genuine you are. Doesn't matter how passionate or romantic you are. none of that will ever compensate for a really impressive list of credentials. When in the world did Love become a math problem instead of a life solution?

Just my thoughts, good people. Just my thoughts.

Don't Be So Focused On Making The Wrong Decision That You Overlook Making The Right One

WAKE UP, WAKE UP, WAKE UP. Today is the day where you stop wrestling with any forms of doubt. It's the day when you look yourself in the mirror, and you accept your reflection for what it is. You accept your flaws, you acknowledge your strengths, and you vow to have them both work together to make you the person you want to be. Excuses are gone with yesterday, and they are forever in your past. It's said that there three types of people in this world: those who watch things happen, those who make things happen, and those who have no idea of what's happening. My advice is to you is that you choose to be the person who makes things happen. Obstacles are only the things a person sees when they take their mind off their goals. STAY FOCUSED. Start something and see it all the way through. Don't be moved by your fears – just do it. Because at the end of the day, if you're wondering what's holding you back, if you're wondering why you aren't where you always saw yourself being, the answer will lie in the face you see each time you look in the mirror.

Just my thoughts, good people. Just my thoughts.

Dream Killers

There's no need to look for approval in everything you do. Your willingness to change, grow, and live abundantly will not always be willingly accepted by those with narrow minds. Don't expect the people who aren't growing to recognize your growth. They'll notice your change solely because it's a painful reminder that they chose to remain the same. You don't need anybody outside of yourself to believe in your dreams in order for them to come true. Don't stop going where you're going in life just because people are stuck at where you were in life. They're so busy judging you that they've forgotten that they need to be living too. Opinions are optional, so if it isn't positive reinforcement or constructive criticism, I don't care to hear it. My mindset remains that every opinion of me won't be included in my definition of me. You may doubt many things in life, but don't ever let somebody's lack of faith make you doubt your dreams. Be confident in what you know is best for you. Dreaming is the first step towards destiny, so if you're headed out on a journey, don't waste time consulting with people who have never left home. Dream killers believe that they can't start until they know, but dream livers understand that you won't know until you start! Be smart, be faithful, and be prepared. Power your dreams beyond those powerless beings that doubt you.

Just my thoughts, good people. Just my thoughts.

About Something Real
Rob Hill Sr.

Dreams And Excuses

Your life will be as hard as you make it. When you make excuses, you turn a puddle of problems into a sea of trouble. You can't keep coming up with reasons as to why you can't do this and why you can't do that. When you see a hurdle, jump over it; it's simple as that. The only things you can't do are the things you say you can't. Just know that God has given you the strength to do all things, no matter how big or how small. When you see quitting as an option, all you've done is made failure a choice. I promise you, trying a little harder will not kill you. In fact, it will make you better. Where there's a will, there's a way. You won't always see the way at first, but if you really want it, you'll gain the vision to make a way. Stop quitting so easily. You can't avoid trying just because things look hard. the bigger the trial, the greater your triumph. The only thing that can stop you is you. An obstacle is nothing but a speed bump to an unstoppable force. Be that unstoppable force, be so determined to succeed that your dreams don't allow you to sleep. The difference between the successful and the unsuccessful are not in their abilities, it's in their level of consistency. Dreams may come to you in your sleep, but they only come true as a result of work. There is nothing that can stop the mission of a mind that's truly made up. There is a prime period of time for opportunity in every season. Don't miss your window, and be prepared to seize your moment. You can't sit back and wait for the next time because there may be no next time. You have to go out and give life your all. Not just on the easy tasks, but on the tasks that require a little blood, more sweat, and a lot of tears. If you want a good life, fight the good fight, and don't stop until you're victorious.

Just my thoughts, good people. Just my thoughts.

Duty Of Disappointment

Disappointment should be as simple to deal with as anger. Anger is so easy because it's a fleeting emotion that can change with a simple smile, but only time fixes disappointment. When it comes to love, it is better to know and be disappointed than to not know and always wonder. Be calm, be strong, and be patient. We need to meet heartbreak and disappointment with courage. We should expect to work for love, but be wise enough to never accept being abused in its name. Rise superior to the trials life presents and never give in to hopelessness or despair. Disappointment is the nurse of wisdom, but if handled the right way, it can play doctor to your healing. However, your healing comes with a process, and that process begins with understanding and acknowledgement. Everyone is not the same. Give people a fair chance. Sure hurt people hurt people but mature people heal people if given the opportunity. Love is work because it's life's greatest offering. Many will speak it, but few will feel it. Every one of us is granted the easiness of lust, but few are patient enough to be rewarded through the disappointments of love. Let downs should be lessons, not excuses to stay down. Be wise. Let the duty of disappointments and pain kill your pride without allowing them to steal your heart.

Just my thoughts, good people. Just my thoughts.

Dying Inside But Outside You Looking Fearless

We have to be so tough in this world. Never showing any vulnerability. We laugh when we really feel like crying. We go through all the motions, just to avoid the reality of our emotions. We aren't meant to go through life numb or falsely feeling protected in our glass houses. Certain things happen because that's the essence of how we learn, through feeling – be it joy or pain. It's easy not to care, but don't suck the life out of your body refusing to feel, because it doesn't help you or those around you. If you choose to care less in hopes to be in a position of power, then never expect somebody to care more, because that's not how love works. Growing hurts, but pain promotes maturity. Happiness and love are not just ideas; they are realities. I pray entirely too much for them not to be.

Just my thoughts, good people. Just my thoughts.

Elements Of Greatness

Be unforgettable. Live in such a way that people's lives are forever changed when they meet you. Do so in such a fashion that it can't be duplicated. Be treasured. Don't let anybody just take up space in your life. If they aren't motivating you to do better, they'll be distracting you from getting better. If your life is exactly the same after a person as it was before them, then you've wasted your time. If you have to question what somebody brings to the table, then you probably shouldn't be eating with them. Be passionate. You have to live your passion. Part time effort will never get you full time success. A life without passion is a life that is lacking. You have to believe in something, someday. Be ever growing. With every situation, no matter good or bad, you have to find a way to be better from it. Getting older is inevitable, but growth is optional. Live in a way that matures you. Be ambitious. To have "drive" is to have a sense of purpose. The essence of ambition is found when you recognize that you are on a mission. Success embodies three aspects that can never be compromised: love, passion, and growth. When you have these, you attract greatness.

Just my thoughts, good people. Just my thoughts.

Embrace Expectations

Every person you choose to keep in your life should be contributing something to your life. Whether it's the person you go to for a smile, the person you feel safe with, or the one person you can trust and depend on. Some believe that if you have no expectations, then you get no disappointments. But they don't realize that when you deny the need for expectation, you also fail to set the standard. When you expect nothing, you're usually left with nothing. When you expect or accept anything, all you'll get is anything, and that usually consists of everything you don't want. If you're in situations that do nothing for your life, be wise and do something better with your time. Anybody who's in love claiming that they love with no expectations is lying. Don't be so pressed on playing it safe and not getting hurt that you settle for being miserable. Of course, you can't expect the most of everybody, but if you can't expect anything from those closest to you, then why are they close to you? It's realistic to expect everybody in your life to add value. If they don't, it'd be wise to subtract them.

Just my thoughts, good people. Just my thoughts.

An Excuse To Be Miserable

Don't make a thousand excuses for zero actions. Failure defined in its simplest form is saying you can't do something before you've even tried. If you're tired of being sick and tired, then stop being sick and tired. It's really that simple. Some people complain so much that all they have space to receive is more pain. You can't run from your problems, they don't have to chase you because they're ahead of you. In order for you to have a breakthrough, you have to face what's in front of you. Insanity may be doing the same things over and over expecting a different result. But stupidity is being naïve enough to think things won't get worse. Situations in your life won't change until you start changing. Stop looking for excuses to be miserable and start looking for reasons to smile. Life may be giving you the roughest times it ever has, but moping around isn't fighting back – that's giving up. You may be frustrated, you may be depressed, and you may feel discouraged. But you don't have time to quit. The hardest part in any race is the finish, but you have to be strong enough to see it through. Cry, scream, and fight, do whatever you have to do, just don't quit. If the bad really outweighed the good in your life, you'd be dead right now. Find reasons to be thankful, not excuses to be miserable.

Just my thoughts, good people. Just my thoughts.

An Exercise In Futility

All of our daily choices reflect who we are and profoundly influence the life we'll lead. Each choice and each decision add another piece to the puzzle of our lives. However, few of us are in position to see the bigger picture, so we're working against ourselves placing all the right pieces in the wrong puzzles. We're investing our time, energy, and emotions into condemned property hoping to see some kind of return, and we wonder why our hearts are bankrupt. I think we need to understand that every rag does not have a rise to riches. Some rags are just supposed to stay rags. Sure, I love to fantasize about roses growing from concrete, but when given a choice, I'm planting my seeds in fertile land and not in some parking lot. Yet, so many of us are placing pieces of ourselves in puzzles that were never meant to be completed, people we never meant to love, and relationships that aren't relatable. You can tell a thousand people to go get what they deserve, but if they have no idea what that is, you'll just end up with a thousand people settling for what they already have. In essence what I'm saying is, everything and everybody you feel you deserve, won't necessarily deserve you, so don't get mad when people misuse and abuse your love and time, especially when you didn't require them to earn it.

Just my thoughts, good people. Just my thoughts.

About Something Real
Rob Hill Sr.

Experience Increases Faith And Decreases Fears

Worrying will never overcome your fears, only prayer and action can do that. Look yourself in the mirror and be confident that you've learned from your past. To love and to fear pain is to live and fear death. You can't control when either comes so live boldly; life doesn't stop just because you do. When your fear of not being happy becomes more important than your fear of being hurt, your outlook on life will change. Fear is not a legitimate excuse to sell yourself short. You've been hurt before, but you survived. Be courageous knowing you made it through, not scared because it happened. Starting over is hard because most fear what they don't know, but you have to believe in what experience has taught you. You know the games, you know how to spot a fool, and you know you have to protect your heart. Trust what you know, don't fear the things you don't because you can't control that. Fools trust fear because they understand being miserable, but the wise take chances because they know they deserve joy. Long lasting love and happiness may be foreign to you, but it's not impossible for you. You've played the fool, but you learned. You've been hurt, but you're stronger. You've met good enough, and now you're greater than! Every successful lover has had to be a great fighter because love isn't easy. When experience has truly taught you, fear can't beat you and doubt won't stop you. Faith over fears, love over all.

Just my thoughts, good people. Just my thoughts.

49

Faith is Greater than Fear

Keep fighting. Keep persevering. Keep living. Conquerors move in faith, cowards are bullied by fear. If you're still breathing, God is not through with you yet. You may feel like you're losing, but you waking up this morning is evidence that you haven't lost. Be encouraged. God has the final say in every situation regarding you. It may be hard to see, but you are not alone, and your efforts are not in vain. Every failure is a steppingstone, every trial is a gateway to triumph, and every fall is new strength to rise again. Don't be fooled into believing God doesn't want you to live abundantly. He wants more for you than you could ever imagine for yourself. However, if He says no to it, your life has no use for it. Fear binds you; faith frees you. Allow your faith to stretch past the confines you've placed on your reality. For when you're truly on the road to your destiny, speed bumps may slow you down, but nothing will stop you. Not your job, not your family, and especially not your "friends." So be strong, be fearless, and be faithful. The storm doesn't last forever.

Just my thoughts, good people. Just my thoughts.

Face Value

Don't drive yourself crazy over analyzing things. Stop looking for hidden meanings and messages that aren't really there. When people speak, listen to their words. Don't try to twist and turn them just so you like what you hear. If their actions consistently show that they don't care, address it. But if nothing changes, I suggest you exit. Stop making excuses for people who aren't trying to make a way for themselves. If he won't commit, it's because he genuinely doesn't want to commit. If she won't trust you, it's not because she can't trust, she's just too insecure to try. And if you let the fears of an ugly past block you from the possibilities of a beautiful future, you're not just settling, you're losing. Most frustration comes from trying to understand things that we weren't meant to. Sometimes you just have to take things at face value. When you really want something, you do what you have to do to get it. It's that simple. Looking too deep into things can have you searching for nothing and ignoring the something that's right in front of your face.

Just my thoughts, good people. Just my thoughts.

51

Family, Friends, And Snakes

If you and somebody ALWAYS agree, one of you is lying. Don't let your pride fool you into believing that everybody with an opinion is a hater. The person speaking up probably just cares about you enough to dare you to be better. Respect and cherish those who challenge you in the midst of your crisis, their eyes may see you as a contestant, but their faith recognizes you as a champion. The wise are mindful of the people they surround themselves with because they know every family member isn't familiar and every friend isn't friendly. Jealousy, pessimism, and contentment are diseases that are passed around more than the common cold. Life is already hard enough. It's designed to take us through ups and downs. It gives us battles to fight in hopes that we gain the tools to keep our hearts, eyes, and minds focused on winning the war. Don't allow the depressed, misguided, and unmotivated people to hurt you, drag you down, and allow you to lose sight of your direction in life. Misery loves company, and her pity parties always sell out. Cut the dead weight before you become it in other areas of your life.

Just my thoughts, good people. Just my thoughts.

Favor And Faith

Never let your doubts outshine your dreams. You have to believe in yourself for yourself. Success appreciates support, but its primary requirement is the faith you have in you. There are a million people out there eager to tell you what you can't do, be confident enough to have a trillion reasons as to why you can. When people doubt you, it only puts limitations on them. But allow those same doubts to place motivation in you. Be careful whom you share your dreams with, when people realize they can't reach theirs; they'll do whatever they can to steal yours. Some feel like if you succeed, then it means that they can't. So instead of chasing their own successes, they'll try to block you from yours. However, when people pray on your downfall, it only expedites theirs. God does not answer the prayers of the spiteful. Favor ain't fair, and neither is success. If you aren't willing to give up what I gave then, you won't get what I have. Sacrifice is solemn. Embrace who you are. Everybody won't understand you because everybody can't be you. You are you for a divine reason. Take your dreams to places the doubters can only fantasize about. Let their fear be the constant fuel to your faith knowing that what God has for you is for you and only you.

Just my thoughts, good people. Just my thoughts.

53

Find Acceptance

There is a fine line between love and dysfunction. There is a distinct difference between passionate and crazy. Beware of the little things you find yourself doing to confuse either of the two. Acceptance is such a huge factor in people's lives today. The ability to accept something, be it good or bad, is pivotal when it comes to change and growth. Accept that what you want may not be what you need. Accept that everything you love won't always love you back. Accept that sometimes when you give, you're giving to somebody who doesn't know how to receive. They reject you out of their own neglect. Sometimes the things we're forced to accept can really hurt, but it's not the end of the world. New love does not erase old scars. It just gives you more reasons to appreciate what you've experienced. If there are some things you just refuse to accept, don't be surprised when you're blocked from taking that next step in life. Don't let your pride dig a hole your reality can't climb out of. Learn to stop when you're ahead. Don't allow your emotions to have you making stupid decisions; you have to be smarter than that. So many people get caught up in their perception of love that they forget to see the deception in lust. Don't be fooled by the bliss, don't be fooled by the butterflies, don't get caught up in the fairy tale. If it's real, there won't be anything to force. Dwelling on certain things won't do anything, but make bad situation worse.

Come to terms with the fact that what you think you want will never compare to what God knows you need.

Just my thoughts, good people. Just my thoughts.

Forgive

When you lose the ability to forgive people, God loses his desire to forgive you. Learn how to let go and to move on. It may be hard to do it, you may need time to do it, but don't let anything stop you from getting it done. Bringing up the past every time you get angry is not forgiveness; it's childish resentment. Spite and bitterness will never propel you the same way that they can postpone you. Don't allow anger to block your heart from the healing that it needs. If you say you're over something, then actually be over it. Don't claim to have moved on when you're still harboring secret feelings. Communicate and get your issues out in the open so you can find common ground towards solving the problem. Having the same arguments over and over is a clear sign of no progress, and that's usually because one side is holding on to something they should've already let go. When you argue solely to prove points, it's because pride is involved. But when finding a solution is the goal; it's called a discussion. They say most people don't have a problem with forgiving; they just don't want you to forget that they forgave. However, when you feel the need to keep track of the times that you forgave somebody, it's probably because you never really did. Forgive in a way that allows you to not only move on but to move forward, regardless of whether its forgotten or not.

Just my thoughts, good people. Just my thoughts.

Fixed Fear

Sometimes the worst thing you can do is be scared. Life is a roller coaster, one minute you're up, and the next minute you're down. However, for every loss, there is a gain. There is nothing you'll be called to go through that isn't designed to benefit you. Most of us don't have time to be scared; being afraid puts things further away. Don't let anything stop you from getting closer to your dreams. You don't have time to sit and wait for some false courage that the world tells you will just come one day. Things happen when you make them, things change when you make them, and fears flee when you make them. It's all on you. The longer a fear is avoided, the stronger that fear becomes. You transition from a fear of getting hurt to a fear of getting close to people at all. Listen, life doesn't stop happening just because you fear what's next. You have to put it in your mind that you can handle whatever is handed to you. Life will hurt you, and people will hurt you. There is no avoiding that, but nothing can hurt you worse than your own fears. It's not about what you learn; it's about what you apply. That's why knowing better requires you to do better. Some things you just never want to experience again, but if you don't learn the principles you'll have to repeat the lesson. You have to master disaster. Learn how to take a few hits and still bounce back stronger. If you have bad days, you're ignoring God's grace. Don't take time for granted. Know what experiences to keep and know which ones to throw out. Everything you hold on to should be to better you. Don't let you fears interfere with your favor. Put your potential before your past. Don't just sit on situations thinking they'll just fade away; you can ignore a single raindrop, but don't be surprised when you're hit with a storm. You can be scared, or you can be prepared. It's your choice. Just know the fearful don't succeed until they become the faithful. Fix your fears.

Just my thoughts, good people. Just my thoughts.

Forward Progress

We have to remove the past from our present. Regardless of how much it hurt, how disappointed we were, or what time was wasted. The hate, anger, and pain that we're holding on to in our hearts aren't worthy of the self-destruction, the walls, the barriers, and the limitations we bring to our souls. Pride postpones prosperity; the moment we decide to let things go is when we learn to let ourselves grow. Any heart filled with animosity, bitterness, and revenge has no room for love. When the wise say forgive and forget, it is not an invite to repeat the offense. It just releases all power from the offender. Though forgiveness does not change your past, willingly enduring the process will enlarge your future. Harboring resentment is like eating poison and waiting for the other person to die; you're only hurting yourself. Life is already short as it is; don't kill your spirit refusing to move on.

Just my thoughts, good people. Just my thoughts.

59

Free Your Mind

We are creating our lives with our thoughts. The pessimist, the optimist, the free spirits, we're all creating the situations and occurrences of our day-to-day lives with each thought. The admissions of stress, the invitations to despair, and the unconscious submission to "impossibilities" are self-imposed prisons. We attract whatever we choose to give our attention to, whether it's wanted or unwanted. We have to work on changing our thoughts into a more positive direction. When a negative thought enters our mind, we have to catch it, stop ourselves, and turn it into something positive. Simple practices like this can reposition us and change our lives around. We flirt with frustrations and party with pity just to get nowhere. Instead of being the victim in our lives and letting things happen to us, we have to realize that it is us and us alone that are responsible for what happens in OUR lives. Free your mind and the rest will follow. ;).

Just my thoughts, good people. Just my thoughts.

Friends

One of the worst things in friendship is seeing your friend hurt and knowing you can't do anything about it. It's tough caring about somebody you can't help. It's hard loving somebody you can't trust. And it's the worst thing knowing somebody you care about deserves so much more than what they think they want. We can't always protect our friends and loved ones the way we wish we could, but we're still required to be there. We won't always approve of every decision our friends make, but friendship is more about loyalty than it is approval. Love is more about trust than it is about bliss. And understanding is more about acceptance than it is comprehension. Friendship is about the little things that people do to let you know they're in your corner. It's a different kind of support; it's a "text you at random times just to say I believe in you" kind of support. Few people understand what it really means to be there for somebody. Everybody trying to build you up will not be built to stay around; some people can't handle being there for your struggles. Stay clear of the fair weather people. Anybody can enjoy the sun, but who's going to be around when the rain shadows your parade? Most people can't keep a friend because they don't know how to be one. Instead of looking for ways to help you be a better friend, they'll find reasons to call you a phony one. There's a balance that comes with friendships that has to be maintained at all times and three things keep it together: honesty, loyalty, and love. If you know your friend needs you, be there for them, not there to judge them. Support the people who support you and let them know you care. Push your friends to consistently improve. If your friendships don't challenge you, they can't better you. The essence of a friend is knowing you have somebody there, somebody to trust, and somebody to lean on. If you don't have that friend, it's probably because you aren't that person. When you become a better friend, you get better friends.

Just my thoughts, good people. Just my thoughts.

Get Closer To Your Dreams

It's ironic how so many of us are always getting ready to live but never living. We're waiting for life to give us the clue, but when given, we're never getting it. Realize that whether we're living the best times or the worst times, this is our only time, and the wise make the best of it. Our circumstance and mistakes can set back our position, but that should only give us conquerors a greater focus our mission. If you have the ability to dream, the courage to believe, and the guts to make it happen, nothing can stop you. It doesn't matter what you're trying to do. Good people wait on opportunity, great people create opportunity. Take a chance and invest in your future, and believe in your dreams, because you're the only one who can make them happen in a way that they will last. And you can live the dream a thousand people picked for you, but all that leaves you with is regret and a thousand new haters because you're living what they couldn't. The fruition of your dreams will always reflect the effort you've invested in them. Good people, if you waste your money, then you've only lost some money. But if you waste your time, you've lost part of your life. The only way to seize the moment is to be in the moment, stop letting life pass you by waiting on the perfect timing because no matter how long you wait, time never will.

Just my thoughts, good people. Just my thoughts.

Get Out Of Your Way

Sometimes we stare so long at the door that's closing that we fail to see the one that's opened. We don't realize that it's impossible to catch our blessings if our hands are full with mess. We have to let it all go; don't set yourself up holding on to something that has already let go of you. Life is far too short to be chasing your past; all you're doing is wasting the present while getting further away from your future. Let go of "what was" so you can open up to "what is" and be strong enough to accept the chance of those two being entirely different. Let your memories remember love, but let go of the resentment because it only remembers regret. If you care, then speak up. If it's valuable, take care of it. And if you want more, give more. Lose your pride for your love; don't lose love over your pride. The only way your past can block your future is if you're standing in the way.

Just my thoughts, good people. Just my thoughts.

Gift of Time

The most important thing you can give anybody is your time. Some people would actually prefer time with you instead of love from you. Your love is fulfilling, but your time shows appreciation. Somebody thinks so highly of you that all they want to do is to be in your presence. Don't make them feel like that's a crime. I know times get busy, but you have to learn how to juggle being busy and doing what's necessary. Work will always be there; love does not come with that same promise. Sure love never dies, but love does not have to die in order to leave you. Stop taking things for granted. Assess your life. Do the people that really matter know how important they are to you? If they don't, fix it. Make time to put a smile on your partner's face. You don't have to do something extravagant, just be thoughtful every once in a while. Quality time is undivided attention. We're all guilty of cell phone pleasures, but you'll still live if you turn it off for an hour or two. Start giving the people in your life the time they deserve. Your partner should not have to threaten to leave you just for you to notice them. If you can't make time for that somebody special, expect the time you take for granted to be used by somebody else. Smarten up before you miss out.

Just my thoughts, good people. Just my thoughts.

Give And Take Relationships

Be mindful of people who act as if your world should revolve around them. We all enjoy helping our loved ones, but make sure your relationships have balance. People should feel appreciative of your time, not entitled to it. You need people around you that give just as much, if not more, than they take. There's nothing worse than knowing you're there when everybody needs a shoulder to cry on and watching them disappear when it's your turn. You've got to get out of the one-sided relationships. Be it with your friends, your family, or the one you love. Happiness comes from balance. If you're constantly giving to people who could care less about giving back, you'll always feel lonely. You can't break yourself down trying to hold everybody up. You have to understand that what you may see as helping could actually be hindering. There's a difference between being dependable and being used. Just because you're there for a person all the time doesn't give them the right to take you for granted. If you're down, I'll help you get up, but if you don't want to help yourself, there's nothing I can do for you. Now of course, we all want the equal bond that works 50/50 but it's not always possible. On the days when you only have the strength to give 30, you're going to need a partner that's built to give you 70. If you can't let your guard down around them, they're probably somebody you don't need around you. Never allow anybody or anything to give you less than you would give yourself.

Just my thoughts, good people. Just my thoughts.

Give, Give, Give

The highest expression of love is to give without expecting. The concept may be hard to accept, but the principle is necessary to understand. Give a little, even on the days where you feel like everyone around you only wants to take. Give, not because of what you may get back, but give solely because you know it's the right thing to do. At times it can seem as if we're too nice to people who don't deserve it, but they're actually the ones who need it the most. When you're mad, depressed, or frustrated, you're probably not the easiest person to love. But during those times, that's when you need love the most. Give trust and give love, just be wise enough to give it in increments. There should be levels to everything. First, you give a person your attention, then some of your time, then some of your affection, and then they get your heart. You don't give it all in the beginning. Make your effort match the moment, if things are still early and you're undecided, be 100% honest, not 100% transparent. The beginning of relationships requires more logic than emotion. You assess the quality and character of the person and decide whether they deserve you emotionally. You give in proportion to what is deserved, not according to what you feel at the moment. If you know somebody has worked for your love, don't hesitate to give them your effort, even on the bad days. Most of what you give is reflected in what you get; thus, the concept of Karma. When you give lies, you don't get trust. When you give hate, you don't get love. When you give no effort, you don't get success. Learn the importance of giving and learn the value of service. The only way you can be taken advantage of is when you give the advantage away. Don't let emotions block your vision. The key to giving is knowing who is truly deserving. When you give to the undeserving, you're asking to be unappreciated. When you give to the selfish, expect to be taken for granted. But when you give to love, expect to be cherished, expect to be adored, and expect to be loved back. There are no perfect days, but when you give the right way, you become more equipped to handle the difficult ones. Luke 6:38 "Give and you will receive. Your gift will return to you full - pressed down, shaken together to make room for more, running over, and poured into your lap. The amount you give will determine the amount you get back".

Just my thoughts, good people. Just my thoughts.

The Glass House

Every time I let my guard down, all I ever see is solid walls. It's like we're all living in our own fish tanks. How do we learn to let other people in? I wonder at what level of maturity does the opportunity to be vulnerable become a strength and not a weakness. Never loving can't possibly hurt as much as loving and losing because you haven't experienced it to know...right? Most of us are living secure lives in mansions of emotional solitude. We invite our guests into our estates, but make them sleep in a tent on the lawn. As if to say, I want you close enough to watch, but not so close that you can touch me. When our hearts scream "I'm sorry or I care about you", the world forces our mouths to say "it is what it is". We all want the same things, complain about the same things, but are stuck playing the same game.

Just my thoughts, good people. Just my thoughts.

Gratitude

Take nothing for granted. Learn everything you can, every chance that you can, from everyone that you can even if it's what not to do. Be grateful for every opportunity presented, your big break won't come every day, but you can start by taking advantage of the little cracks along the way. It is foolish to know that you have everything you need and still complain about a lack in the things you want. Some of us are asking God for mansions, and we haven't even taken care of the temple he gave us at birth. The more thankful you are with the things God has already given you, the more things he will bless you with to be thankful for. Sometimes the hardest math to add up is the one in which we're asked to count our own blessings. Life isn't always about what we like or dislike. It really comes down to doing what needs to be done, you may not be elevated to cloud nine everyday, but at least you'll be on the stairway to greatness. Be blessed and be thankful, be humble and be grateful. Take nothing for granted because nothing is promised.

Just my thoughts, good people. Just my thoughts.

Growing Hurts

A friend of mine told me that people sometimes create this fantasy world as an emotional crutch to get away from things. We get scared of life, so we slowly kill our souls refusing to live it. There comes a time when the same old things keep bringing the same old results, and it's just not working for us anymore. We forced to step it up in areas of life that we've constantly ignored or made excuses for. We keep waiting and saying things will work themselves out, and the reality is, things don't just work themselves out. God does once we are faithful and accept our assignment. The walls, the gates, the barriers to keep the heartaches, rejection, and disappointment out are the very things that confine you from really living. The people who live life in fear of failure will never meet success, the people who hide from pain will never be found by love, and those who refuse to change, unconsciously refuse to grow. So yeah, growing hurts, but I'd rather endure the pain of progression than live the rest of my life with regrets.

Just my thoughts, good people. Just my thoughts.

Grown People

Don't claim to be grown when it's convenient. Handling your business is your responsibility. It's not something to complain or brag about because it's what you're expected to do. It pains me that some people still think with adolescent mindsets. It's like they know they can't be young all their life, so they decide to be immature forever. You have to grow up at some point. Certain mistakes by little girls turn into grown woman problems just like little boy decisions have grown man consequences. If you have responsibilities that you refuse to be responsible for, then I have no respect for you. Adults are accountable for their actions. If you're quick to speak up to get credit, but slow to fess up when being corrected, then you're still a child. If you're not striving to be the best you possible, then you're losing because being good enough just doesn't cut it. You can't change people, you can't change your circumstance, and you can't change your past. But you can change yourself, you can change your attitude, and you can change your life. It all starts and ends with your willingness to do so. Age defines time, not maturity; so in the midst of growing older, don't forget to grow up.

Just my thoughts, good people. Just my thoughts.

Habits

Most of the things we do are without reason; we just do them because it's what we've always done. However, you'll never get new results out of old habits. When you go the places you've always gone, you'll see the people you've always seen, doing the same things they've always done. So, stop dating using the same methods that have failed you countless times. No longer invest your time in the people who've done nothing but misuse it. There's only so long you can justify "doing you" without having results for anything you've done. Only a fool expects different results from doing the same old things. It's pointless to complain about a lack of change if you're not trying to engineer any for yourself. You're never too busy to improve upon yourself and your habits. Start investing real time into habits of productivity and get rid of those destructive ways. If you want to grow, these three things have to die: your old habits, your old way of thinking, and your old self-image. If you've made a habit of making excuses, then you've also made a commitment to failure. Let go of habits like procrastination, lying, & improper planning to welcome habits like punctuality, order, and diligence. If you're going to have a habit, be wise enough to have it make you better. The only difference between those who succeed and those who fail is in their habits. It's not what you do every once in a while; it's what you do day in and day out that makes the difference.

Just my thoughts, good people. Just my thoughts.

Happiness And Joy

People can only take from you what you allow them to. Those who you feel just want to see you down, disrupt your peace, and break your heart only have the rights you've given them to these intangibles. Seek joy over happiness because there is a divine difference in the two, happiness is a mere emotion, but joy is an attitude of the heart. People may be able to steal your happiness because it's a temporary sentiment, but the day a person is allowed to rob you of your joy better be the day you died refusing to give it to them. We have to learn to focus on our joys instead of our concerns; we can't let circumstance and sorrow mute the song in our souls. Yes, the world can take your stuff, but it's not entitled to your spirit. When it comes to matters of the heart, some may be cool with compromising their happiness, but no one should ever sacrifice their joy. Even the hardest of times can offer reasons to be happy, but true joy resonates with peace: peace in your heart, peace in your spirit, and peace of mind. And nobody can take that joy from you because nobody deserves that more than you.

Just my thoughts, good people. Just my thoughts.

Having A Strong Circle

Make sure the circle you're in is growing with you and not trying to close on you. Most people can't get ahead because they're holding on to people who lack ambition. You'll never reach the mountaintop if you have to carry everybody on your back. Have people in your life that can inspire you, but still know how to motivate their self. If you're trying to go places in life you, you need people around you who have actually been somewhere. It'll be hard to follow a dream if all you have is closed minds in your circle. What you recognize as real, they see as impossible. Some people you'll just have to be cool with from a distance. You don't need certain people in your everyday life. Not everybody will understand what you want to do and where you're trying to go, and if you're not careful you'll get distracted. My mindset is this: You can't antagonize me and influence me at the same time. So if you're not concerned with helping me, I'm not concerned with you judging me. Don't get discouraged thinking that things will never work out; things begin to work out once you start to put work in. Show me a problem, and I'll show you a promise. There is no trial too big for you to triumph. Understand that delayed does not mean denied. When the timing is right, what you want will coincide with what you need. Just make sure your circle isn't in the way of that.

Just my thoughts, good people. Just my thoughts.

Healing The Hurt

It isn't always easy to move on from situations that you've invested a lot of yourself into. Some people would rather break up to make up than to break it down and make something real. As sure as the sun rises after the night, there is healing after heartbreak. Pain is the biggest distracter to purpose. You have to stay focused in the midst of your fears. Happiness isn't a fallacy some optimist drew up; it's a reality you experience through sacrifice. There's only so long you can sweep certain things under the rug. Covering your problems is not healing them; it's hiding from them. The hurt that comes from knowing you ignored all the warning signs stings harder than the hurt that comes from any lie. Sometimes the worst wounds are the kind you can't see because many of the best smiles are hiding some of the worst pain. Learn to give people fair chances. Maybe you couldn't stop the past from hurting you, but you don't have to block the future from healing you. Sure, hurt people hurt people, but healed people can heal people when given the chance. Stop using laughter to hide the tears and toughness to mask your fears. Heal the hurt before it hinders your heart.

Just my thoughts, good people. Just my thoughts.

The Heart

Anything that hurts you has the ability to teach you. However, if it continues to hurt you, it's because you haven't learned your lesson. Allow your emotions to drive you, just be wise enough to know when they're driving you nowhere. Pay attention to warning signs, you won't find happiness or love down a dead end street. Don't be afraid to follow your heart; nothing in you has a better sense of direction. Just make sure that what you think you're following is really your heart speaking. A lot of people claim to be listening to their heart, but few recognize how it speaks. Your heart will tell you to be loving, forgiving, and kind. It won't tell you to be stupid, abused, and desperate. Your heart speaks from your needs; your flesh speaks out of wants. You may want something because of the way it makes you feel, but your heart knows what you need. It can recognize if it's actually real. You can't blame your heart for the pain your actions asked for, it didn't lead you there – not listening to it did. You may have to forget what you want in order to remember what you deserve, but if you don't know what you deserve, you'll never be able to get it. The heartless are lifeless. If you want more love, it's going to start with you spreading it.

Just my thoughts, good people. Just my thoughts.

About Something Real
Rob Hill Sr.

Help People Help Themselves

Don't give so much of yourself that when you need you the most, you have nothing left. We're all put into the unique position of being able to help one another at some point in our lives. Though the gift of giving is one of life's greatest pleasures, all giving isn't good and all help isn't beneficial. You'll never really help anyone if you're hurting yourself trying to do it. Give what you can; help when and where you can; and allow God to handle the rest. If your loved one falls down, be there to assist them in walking again. But don't become their permanent crutch. Life isn't designed to be easy for any of us. We all struggle, but the very essence of struggling shows fight, and it implies effort. It's better to endure the pain of progression than to live the rest of your life with regrets. We need the ones we cherish to understand that we'll only be able to help them as much as they desire to help themselves.

Just my thoughts, good people. Just my thoughts.

Hold On

Sometimes the best of people end up with the worst of times. Not because they deserve them, but more so because they were built to handle them. Everything the world sends trying to break you is everything that God intends to use to build you. We all go through hard times, but conquerors get through them stronger, wiser, and better. All complaining does is waste your time; it does nothing to improve your situation. You can't claim the victory if you're too busy playing the victim. Life will always beat you down if you refuse to do anything about it. Stop letting things happen to you and start making things happen for you. Falling down isn't failure – staying down is. Everybody who's ever seen the mountaintops had to start in the valley. Just hold on; where you're going to is bigger than what you're going through. Your success is worth the struggle, and getting "there" may not be easy. But nobody deserves it more than you.

Just my thoughts, good people. Just my thoughts.

Hurt People Hurt People

Be careful of the people you surround yourself with. Jealousy, pessimism, and contentment are diseases that are passed around more than the common cold. Misery loves company, and more often than not, she has a full house. Don't get caught up in the mess. Plain and simple. Life is designed to take us through ups and downs. It gives us battles to fight in hopes that we keep our hearts, eyes, and minds focused on winning the war. Don't allow the hurt people in your life to hurt you, drag you down, and allow you to lose sight of your direction in life. Cut the dead weight before you become it in other areas of your life.

Just my thoughts, good people. Just my thoughts.

I Challenge You

For most people, forgiveness isn't the easiest thing. I do well for the most part, but there are certain areas of my life that I just cannot let go. It's an unhealthy practice, and in reality, the only person that it's hurting is myself. But, at times, I ignorantly feel it's worth it. Facts are facts though. It takes so much time to hold a grudge and harbor anger; it actually takes effort, the kind of effort that leaves you mentally and physically exhausted. Especially when it's with someone you love. We all love differently; we all have our own ways and visions of love and how it should be. But perhaps the most overlooked aspect of love is the "unconditional" part. In the midst of your anger, you have to allow your love for whoever it is to conqueror all else. So I challenge you to love with no reservation, love when it hurts, and love through the pain. Hold onto the truth that the rain doesn't always last. Things aren't always what they seem, so don't cheat yourself out of a diamond just because you felt you were too good to deal with the coal.

Just my thoughts, good people. Just my thoughts.

If It Happens

You can't have an "if it happens, it happens" attitude about everything. Sometimes things are trying to happen, but they can't because you're standing in the way. Open your mind and stop putting your life in a box. Nothing will ever be perfect; it's on you to make it worth it. Don't get so caught up in the fun you're having that you get content with the life you're living. Some of the best fun leads to the worst regrets. Life is not about things just happening; it's about having the courage to make them happen. It's easy to do what you want to do, but are you real enough to do what needs to be done? The foundation of those who consistently struggle is the fact that they overvalue their wants and overlook their needs. If the weekend is all you have to look forward to, then that says something significant needs to change in your life. You have to be able to say no, you have to be wise enough to "sit one out" here and there. Life is less about getting to the top and more about knowing how to stay there. You'll be old a lot longer than you'll be young, don't let 5 years of fun ruin your chance at 50 years of fortune. Start living now in ways that get you eager about the future. Live so productively today that tomorrow works for itself.

Just my thoughts, good people. Just my thoughts.

Ignoring Obvious Things

Never ignore the things you can't cut off. Especially when it comes to your heart, your feelings, and your thoughts. At times emotions can be annoying, but trust that they're there to better you, not to upset you. Don't use logic to dismiss your gut feelings; allow your intelligence to support your intuition. Avoiding the truth may seem like the safe option, but it's actually the option you choose when you want to meet disappointment. Don't believe the lies; what you don't know CAN hurt you, especially when you ignore the chances you were given to find out. When your heart tells you it's time to go, be smart and leave. Sometimes the obvious things are the hardest to find simply because we're constantly overlooking them. Holding on to pieces of happiness may seem more attractive than being alone, but when the relationship breaks; knowing you settled pieces of happiness will be what hurts the most. Seek the truth and be prepared to accept what you find. At times it may hurt you, but just because it hurts you doesn't mean it should break you. Be wise and let the pain you conquer come together to complete you, because ignoring it will only tear you down and deplete you. So save yourself some time, don't ignore the obvious things, they're right in front of your face for a reason.

Just my thoughts, good people. Just my thoughts.

In Order To Heal Your Body, You Have To Heal Your Heart

I think in the midst of protecting our hearts from all the pain and hurt, we've inadvertently blocked out the love and happiness. So many of us contribute the way we live and date to the events of our past. It's nothing wrong with learning from our past, but they have to be the kind of the lessons that benefit our future. We have to be truthful enough with ourselves to confront issues. People tend to ruin their happiness before it is even reached. Just because things don't happen how we planned them, doesn't mean they aren't happening how God designed them. Let's get it together.

Just my thoughts, good people. Just my thoughts.

Integrity, Honesty, Truth

Those who do right have a clear understanding in the value of integrity, honesty, and truth. They know that it takes a lot less time to do things right than it does to explain why you did them wrong. They recognize that integrity comes in your willingness to tell yourself the truth, while honesty is your ability to tell the truth to others. You're a liar if you think being honest is telling the truth only when people can find out. The essence of integrity is doing the right thing, even if nobody is watching. Just because a person can't validate whether you've lied, doesn't give you the right to be a liar. A person of many secrets is a person of many lies; they've just learned to do it without speaking. Some people try to be perfect, some people try to be different, but wise people just try to do right. They understand that doing right is the perfect way to be different. Value honesty and have integrity. The truth stands out, but the truth should be the standard.

Just my thoughts, good people. Just my thoughts.

Keep Fighting

Don't wait until it's too late to start helping yourself. You can't keep brushing things off like nothing affects you because sooner or later, you won't even be able to recognize yourself. Handle situations while you have the chance to. Ignoring your problems will not make them disappear. You'll never be able to solve every issue in your life, but it's easier to face one at a time than it is to fight a closet full of skeletons. The problem isn't that there are problems; the problem is expecting life to be perfect and thinking that having problems is a problem. Put some people around you that you can lean on. If you feel like you can't trust anybody, ask yourself if you can be trusted. Turn your wounds into wisdom and learn how to prosper through your problems. When you find out why you're living, you'll always know how to live. You may feel yourself breaking down, but that's a sign that you're gaining ground toward your breakthrough. Hard times make strong people. You may be hurt, but damaged people are vivacious; they know they can survive. Stay encouraged. If you cry every time the sun leaves, your tears will block you from seeing the stars.

Just my thoughts, good people. Just my thoughts.

86

Learning Through Losing

Sometimes life makes it seems like the good people deserve to end up with the hardest times. However, you should never feel defeated by that fallacy. You may get tired, you may get weary, and you may even think about quitting. But you have to realize that the answers to your prayers are often waiting for you in the presence of your problems. You can't conquer the world from the confines of your comfort zone. You will endure hard times, you will have to sacrifice, and you will take a few losses. But there are valuable lessons in defeat. You learn to persevere, you learn persistence, and you learn the process of progression. The only way to appreciate being at the top is having a humble understanding of what it took to get there. Life will never give you the triumph without the trials, and if it does, prepare for tribulation. Quitting may be a thought in your mind, but it should never be an option in your life. Move forward and move confidently. You are where you are for a reason. Times may be rough, and you'll get a few headaches trying to find your way, but your future is worth the temporary frustration. So press on.

Just my thoughts, good people. Just my thoughts.

A Letter to Those Who Wait For Tomorrow

Dear procrastinator: What is so wrong with today? What's so wrong with taking advantage of the 'now' versus waiting for the comforts of 'tomorrow'? What is it you're scared of? Our potential is limitless, but the fears of our own strength and power can prevent us from meeting it. Doubts and fear cause us to second guess our every move and keep us from pressing forward. The last thing we need is another excuse to wait for tomorrow. It's not enough to just have potential; life requires much more. It requires self-confidence, and the will power to have an invested interest in ourselves and TODAY. To see a new challenge in each day and rise to the occasion. To see ourselves as the Kings and Queens God called us to be. Not just today, but everyday. Each one of us has potential, but refusing to use it makes having it useless. Stop wasting today waiting on tomorrow.

Just my thoughts, good people. Just my thoughts.

Life Affects

Everybody who knows better will not want to do better. Some people are more concerned with "doing them" than they are with "doing right." Don't assume that just because somebody is aware that they're wrong means that they care to be right. See things and people as they truly are, not just how you want them to be. Everybody doesn't have big dreams, you may see a person as a giant, but it's pointless if they have the mentality of a midget. Some would rather be chief among the cool kids than champion amongst conquerors. Best of the best should be the goal, not best of the rest. Some people are content with letting "almost" describe them. But in a successful life, almost doesn't count. Watch the things you choose to accept. Temporary approval can lead to long-term denial, especially if you have your eyes closed. The convenient thing at times can seem more appealing than the right thing. But just know that some of the sweetest pleasures bring the worst headaches. Life isn't about doing things the hard/easy way; it's about being wise and patient enough to go with the smart way. Prayer changes things when your actions allow it to. You can't ask for success, but refuse to work. Push yourself and pray for the choices of those around you. Don't feel bad about getting ahead if they chose to stay behind.

Just my thoughts, good people. Just my thoughts.

89

Life...Your Decisions, Your Happiness"

What you decide to do for your life should be your decision, not some conclusion that everybody else came up with for you. It's good to have those that you trust and confide in, but when it's time to make a decision, nobody should be thinking for you. Don't get so caught up in looking for approval that you miss opportunities. When it comes to happiness, most people never get happy because they're too worried about people being happy for them. Nobody has to like what you like in order for you to enjoy it. No one has to treasure what you treasure in order for it to be valuable. It's so important for most people to understand this, especially when it comes to relationships. Be careful what you tell people, it may be something small to you, but people don't forget. When it comes to you, what you do, and who you love, opinions should be taken into consideration. But you have to come up with your own conclusion. Nobody knows what's best for you like you do, and even if somebody did, you won't appreciate knowing until you find out on your own. Live and learn; that's the essence of life. You won't always make the right decisions, but as long as you're breathing, there's nothing you can't bounce back from. Everybody is opinionated, but get people around you who don't always feel like their opinion is needed. Especially when it comes to your mistakes in choosing the people you love. Nobody is perfect; you can't always judge a person off of who you heard they were.

People change every day. However, you can measure a person's willingness to change off of their belief in love. A person who has faith in love also has hope. And anybody with hope will always win, no matter what they face. Start loving who you want to love regardless of who likes it. Start experiencing things you want to experience, regardless of who approves. At the end of the day, 90% of our regrets come from the things we didn't do. There is a difference between being selfish and putting yourself first. Life is easier when everybody is on one accord, but it's not possible. When you're happy, those who matter will be happy for you. Those who aren't, don't need to be around you.

Just my thoughts, good people. Just my thoughts.

Limits Of Your Love

If you put limits on your love, then you put limits on your joy. For love to truly be love, it has no limit. However, when we mix pride with matters of the heart, our ability to love will always be limited. The majority of us could probably love through anything; we're just not naïve enough to love through everything. Most of what we mistake for love really isn't love; it's a deceptive mix of infatuation, manipulation, and bondage. Fools will acknowledge their breaking point as a measure of when to retreat; the wise see their breaking point as a gateway to their breakthrough. Loving with limits doesn't protect you from pain. True pain is felt when your desire for love gets slain by your surrender to fear. Fate determines who we will meet; free choice decides who we will befriend; love gives us no choice in who we fall for. Don't allow the actions of others to force you to limit your love. That's just as dumb as letting the opinions of others limit your life. The way you love may have its limits, but true love is limitless.

Just my thoughts, good people. Just my thoughts.

The Little Things In Life Are Kind Of A Big Deal

The other day I was asked, "When was the best day of your life?" I didn't have an answer. So I thought, and thought, and thought about the best day of my life. Then, I remembered June 13th, 2008. It's the day I looked in the mirror and realized I was proud of myself. The day I accepted my faults, and I accepted not being perfect in anyone's eyes but God's. So, I finally put together the words to answer that question, and my response went something like this, "the best day of my life was when I realized why I was living. It was the day I decided the lessons learned while stumbling to walk, would be the same lessons that kept the air beneath my wings while I soared to fly. It was the day when my desire to be great outshined my desire to be perfect. It was the day when my accomplishments paid homage to my failures. I didn't win the Olympics, didn't win the lottery, I didn't do anything remarkable. It was just a day where for about 10 seconds life made perfect sense.

Just my thoughts, good people. Just my thoughts.

Live For Today

Your today should always compliment your tomorrow. Some of us live life so bent on tomorrow that we let today slip past us. Then, there are others who only think about right now and are blinded as to how today's decisions can and will affect tomorrow's options. It's a thin line to teeter, and sometimes it's hard to maintain a balance. But it's essential to gain one. Make the moves today that leave no chance for regrets tomorrow. There are risks in everything, but take calculated ones. Live for today like there's no tomorrow, but make today's purpose unleash unlimited the possibilities of tomorrow's promise.

Just my thoughts, good people. Just my thoughts.

Logic And Emotion

Don't make permanent decisions based off of temporary emotions. Anger, frustration, and disappointment are confusing emotions, but don't allow a bad mood to ruin a good situation. Neither you nor your partner is perfect. Learn compassion with mistakes. Give them some cushion to mess up, learn from it, and to improve on it. If you aren't patient enough to invest time toward making a good thing a better thing, then you'll never know the joy in having the real thing. Be patient for your treasure. In order to get the diamond, you have to wait the time, endure the pressure, and survive the struggle. If you're one of those people who run with emotions, be prepared to retreat with regrets. Think before you speak. Think before you act. Learn to calm yourself down and think things out. You don't deserve the smooth and easy days if you quit every time things get rough. Stop jumping to conclusions and flying with assumptions before you seek out the facts. You're never sure until you know, and you'll never know until you ask. But if you're too prideful to ask, then be humble enough not to assume. There is no perfect relationship, but just because the situation isn't perfect, doesn't mean it won't be worth the effort. Seeds of faith can blossom into a garden of love when planted in the right soil. What you put into your situation determines what you get out of your situation. You can't give a half and expect to get a whole.

Just my thoughts, good people. Just my thoughts.

Look Ahead

Sometimes we think of our past loves and view them as failures, but we gain wisdom through new love and learn to view the past as a teacher. There is no losing in love, only learning. You learn when to take risk, you learn when to hold on, and most importantly you learn when to let go. You'll never be able to finish the book if you don't close the chapters. If you want to move on, allow the past to be the past as you turn the pages. The pain you've felt in your life was not by chance, it's wasn't a coincidence. It was needed because most people refuse to change anything until it hurts. God knows just how to speak to you, and your life will improve as soon as you learn how to listen. You'll never realize how far you've come if you're still stuck on where you were. Give yourself some credit, you could've quit, but you didn't. You could've made excuses, but instead you made a way. You may not be where you want to be in life, but you can't be on your way if you're wasting time looking backwards instead of forward. God answers all prayers; he just answers them according to what you need, not based on what you want.

Just my thoughts, good people. Just my thoughts.

Love And Fear

We worry too much about all the wrong things. We're not scared of love; we're scared of ourselves. We know love is just as perfect as God designed it to be, but we don't see that the way we love isn't. Love isn't to blame for our imperfections, our lust, or our inability to judge character. Love is innate; it's what we were born with. Fear doesn't understand the divinity in that because it wasn't given to us it was learned; and love isn't to blame for that. We don't realize that worrying will never overcome our fears; only prayer and action can do that. We'll blame love every time we fall short because our pride refuses to look itself in the mirror. To love and to fear pain is to live and fear death. You can't control when either comes, but life goes on. You can stay in the house scared the sky may fall, but I guarantee the roof over your head caves in before God's wonders fail. Fear will never be greater than love because God did not give you that spirit. Yet people will always trust fear because they understand being miserable. Many identify with days of despair; few can be kindred with the peace in delight. The kind of happiness from love that lasts may be foreign, but it's not impossible. Love doesn't just knock you down, its breaks you down. But it has to in order for you to realize that the only way to fly is getting over the fear of falling.

Just my thoughts, good people. Just my thoughts.

Love Is...

I've been trying to finish that sentence. Is love one singular thing or is it a bunch of different things rolled in one? I wonder when my parents say I love you to each other what it translates to. I wonder when people are hurt and say "but I love him/her" what they really mean. When optimists say love conquerors all, does that really mean EVERYTHING? We all love in different ways, but its foundation embodies the same essence, right? We know true love is patient because it bears through any circumstance and never changes. Circumstances change, people change, but true love never changes. No matter what the adversity, true love can bear it. I think the most undervalued part of love is the unconditional part. That's the part of love that understands differences, that's the part that allows YOU to see an orange, ME to see an apple, but US to see fruit. That's what love is...right?

Just my thoughts, good people. Just my thoughts.

98

Love On Valentine's Day

Today is another Monday in the middle of February. It's nothing more than another day to celebrate hearts. Learn to appreciate the day regardless of whether you're actively participating in its festivities or not. Of course you'll hear the "love should be shown everyday" speech, but if people genuinely believed that they wouldn't be complaining about a special day given to those who actually do so. If you're single and Valentine's Day makes you feel lonely, you're not ready for a relationship. Today is a day of love; if you can't embrace that and celebrate yourself, you won't be very successful celebrating with somebody else. The deadline on your happiness was not today. Just because you don't have a valentines doesn't mean God isn't preparing you for a year of love. Ignore the show, and forget the gifts and the flowers. You can choose to make today a significant occasion, or you can treat it like any other day of the year. Do what works for you. Whatever you decide to do, just make sure you realize that its Valentine's Day, not Doom's Day. Life does go on.

Just my thoughts, good people. Just my thoughts.

Love Tips

There's a difference between making love and being blessed with love. We make love when we think it's in our own hands, we're blessed with love when it happens according to God's plan. Just because you put a lot of love into a relationship, doesn't mean you won't get a lot of pain out of it. If it's not meant to be, then it's just not meant to be. Certain relationships are there to be learning experiences. When they fail, your heart should see them as a stepping-stone, not a wrecking block. Use patience to build your emotions up because pride only tears them down. Forge new relationships and stop forcing old ones. Instead of searching for people different from your past, learn to find a better you. There is no controlling love, so stop trying to. It's meant to be enjoyed, not to be controlled. Learn to better the not so pleasant things about yourself, and you'll be better equipped to handle the not so easy days of love. Just know, you can't make love, you can't manufacture emotion, and you can't fabricate passion. Certain things are just too real to be imitated so get that authentic love, not just a replica.

Just my thoughts, good people. Just my thoughts.

Lust And Love

Some of us can't help but to see the best in everybody. We assume that everyone who is physically capable desires to be emotionally available. However, this mindset just isn't true, especially when people won't acknowledge that the same walls lust uses to keep hurt out are blocking love from coming in. Never mix your appetite for life with your lust to live because it will ruin your taste for love. The two may look the same, but they have totally different life spans. Love satisfies your need while lust caters to your wants, and there's no balance in that bond because the relationship is a set up. Love lets you fly while lust lures your fall. Lust happens at first sight, but real love comes with vision and knows it's always good to take a second look. You have to make sure what you're seeing is really what it is – even a blind man can open his eyes. But the wise man understands what he sees. We fall in lust with the potential of a person versus falling in love with the person them self. Don't allow lust to put you in a box of regrets. If you can't decide whether or not your love is lust, then do yourself a favor and let time test it. Once you find out, accept the answer, and don't settle for living in misery just because you're afraid of change. Love yourself enough not to settle for lust.

Just my thoughts, good people. Just my thoughts.

Lying And Other Little Things

In the midst of anger and frustration, a little reassurance goes a long way. Don't be the person who belittles how their partner feels. You don't always have to agree with what they're saying, but don't make them feel small for how they feel. Ease the pain; don't add to it. If you don't care to explain, then you can't complain about being misunderstood. Assumptions succeed when communication fails. Don't use a need for privacy as an excuse to be sneaky. The only time the truth needs explanation is when it comes after a pack of lies. If you get caught up, just tell the truth. You may lose trust, but at least they can respect you for not lying. Never underestimate the actions of a person who's fed up. You may feel irreplaceable, but when a sound mind is made up, it's looking to erase you, not replace you. You can be an amazing person and a great catch. But if you're a lying catch, you deserve to be dropped. Don't ever be so content in your situation that you become careless and nonchalant. Be comfortable, never complacent. There's a toxic laziness that kills all relationships when you start to get complacent. One lie shouldn't end a good relationship, but a consistent liar should. Understand before you judge, listen before you speak, and be honest at all times.

Just my thoughts, good people. Just my thoughts.

Mediocrity

If you're ever comfortable with "good enough" describing any situation in your life, then you're settling. How far you get in life is determined by how hard you're willing to push yourself. Don't get complacent. If you're not making progress, it's because you're not dedicated to the process. You have to take the ups with the downs, the highs with the lows, and still have the courage to keep on going. Life is too short to live off of excuses and regrets. You have to make the best out of this very moment because the next isn't promised. YOU ARE GREAT; not because I'm trying to motivate you, but because you're still here when you could've quit. Don't be fearful, champions excel because they know what failure looks like. Inspiration is a blessing, but it's impossible to sustain success without self-motivation. If you wait for somebody to say you can't do something to get going, you'll always be behind. This is your only chance to live this life. Don't just live. Live LARGE. Don't just dream. Dream BIG. Don't just survive. Be extraordinary and thrive.

Just my thoughts, good people. Just my thoughts.

103

Mind Over Matter

Sometimes our mistakes block us, our failures blind us, and our shortcomings bind us. We put ourselves in this self-confined prison with our thoughts, and we beat ourselves down, over and over again. We think of all the times where we could have done one thing and chose to do another. In life, we all get knocked down, we all fail, and we all lose, but what happens to you doesn't matter half as much as your reaction and what you decide to do about it. You won't always feel happy, you won't always feel attractive, and you won't always feel successful. The key word in that sentence was "feel". Don't be ruled by your emotions, be the ruler of your thoughts. Feed yourself positivity until the word "can't" makes you sick. If you're still breathing, then you should still be learning, still be fighting, still be thankful, and never cease in your quest for wisdom and understanding. Life is not about how fast you run the race; it's about having the courage not to stop.

Just my thoughts, good people. Just my thoughts.

Motivated Patience

If you're asking for opportunity and it comes, it's not the time to rest; it's the time to prove you deserve it. Don't get discouraged by the obstacles you'll face, they're there to strengthen you, not to stop you. Be patient enough not to ruin your blessings before you actually get the chance to be blessed. Change your mindset, recognize when things are bad, but understand that you have a choice in making them better. Don't flirt with frustrations and party with pity just to get nowhere, make your plan bigger than your pain. Keep positive, dependable, and trustworthy people around you. The company you keep influences the opportunities you meet. Don't block your blessings and don't allow the people around you to block your happiness. Decide where you want to be in life and consistently put yourself in positions to get there. Progress begins with an idea, but it ends with complacency. Stay dedicated to your dreams, consistent with your goals, and persistent in your efforts. You may not get what you want, but that doesn't mean you didn't get what you were meant to have.

Just my thoughts, good people. Just my thoughts.

My Body Is My Castle And My Mind Is The Ruler Of This Kingdom

On the day the mirror reflects a face you're not proud of or no longer recognize, what will you do? A person's eyes are the gateway to their soul. New friends, more money, new you, but what happens when you realize all progress isn't moving forward? Or that different doesn't necessarily mean better – it just means different. What does success mean when you lose yourself achieving it? We all want to be better, we all desire to grow and increase in our lives, but in the midst of seeking more we have to maintain our foundation; the morals, beliefs, and values that we came up on. Your life will not always be the Picasso painting you dreamed it up to be, but that doesn't mean it's not a masterpiece. You are YOU for a divine reason.

Just my thoughts, good people. Just my thoughts.

My Needs

I need a change. I need some excitement. I need to wake up in the morning smiling about the possibilities of my day. I need something new. I need a spark. I need the butterflies' new beginnings and welcomed challenges incite. I need the things I want to be seen as needs because the facts are I don't know what I need. I just base the things I think I need off the constant changes of my wants. In reality, what I really need is a new mindset, a refreshed spirit, and a sweet slow dance with humility. I need to take today and make it the best reality it can possibly be in hopes that God will see how grateful I am and graciously bless me with what He knows I need. I've been making decisions based off what I thought I needed for too long, and it just doesn't produce the results I "need" it too. So, today my prayers change from what I think to trusting what He knows. Believing that what God has for me is much more than what I had for myself. My suggestion is you do the same.

Just my thoughts, good people. Just my thoughts.

The Needs Of Consistency

Your life needs consistency. Some things you can't control, God will handle those, but the things you can control are your responsibility. You owe it to yourself to pursue your dreams, reach your goals, and celebrate your life. Do these daily! Your love needs consistency. You can't go back and forth with your emotions. Take a minute and assess whether everything you think you feel is actually real. There is nothing in between about love, either you're in it or you're out! Your peace needs consistency. You have to be confident with your position in life. If you don't like where you are, at least be excited about where you're going. Watch what you do. You can't find peace of mind if your actions are creating a storm! Your trust needs consistency. You can't solve your trust issues trying to date somebody who has them too. Cut the people off who cause stress, confusion, and discontent. If they always have "something" going on in their life, you can trust they'll bring it into yours. A life of abundance requires consistency. Expect to mess up and forgive yourself when you do, but commit to consistently trying to be better. Consistency is everything, and every facet of your life needs it. Without consistency there is no love, there is no peace, and there is definitely no trust.

Just my thoughts, good people. Just my thoughts.

Never Quit

NEVER QUIT. Never give up. Never stop doing what's right. Never grow weary in fighting for the things you stand for and believe in. Life throws us test to see just how much that dream means to you, to see just how much you're willing to sacrifice to attain that goal. The things we're willing to quit on are the things we never really needed or deserved to have. If that relationship is broken due to communication, and we quit talking, then we never deserved that bond. If that job requires extra time, and we quit working, then we never deserved that paycheck. And if life made you lose sight of that dream, and you quit on it, then you never really deserved it. Facts are, we don't always see the ending in the beginning. Yes, we may start something solely looking forward to the end result, but the journey is what gives the ending its value. Detours aren't meant to deter or stop you from your destination. They just give you another route.

Just my thoughts, good people. Just my thoughts.

No Exception

Our entire generation wants that without a doubt love, but I don't see how any of us realistically expect to get it when we don't have that without a doubt faith to know we deserve it. We scream cuffing season as if we're not worthy of companionship year around. We're so plagued by the fallacy that anything wonderful will always be too good to be true. However, when you know you deserve something, there's no such thing as too good to be true. It's called answered prayers. The devi'ls greatest lie was convincing man he didn't exist, but his second has to be convincing us all that good men and women were hard to find. The good aren't hard to find, but the people faithful enough to be blessed with the vision to see them are. I'd always get frustrated when I was told the good guys always finished last until I realized that's what they always save the best for. Anytime I feel discouraged, I patiently remind myself that every worthy treasure deserves its own treasure hunt, and my love is no exception.

Just my thoughts, good people. Just my thoughts.

No Need To Argue

Don't attend every argument you're invited to. Don't address every challenged you're presented with. Just because people want attention doesn't mean they deserve yours. Use some foresight when addressing certain situations. If it won't be a relevant issue tomorrow, there's no sense in stressing it today. Some people will try to piss you off just because you've shown them that they can. However, certain things just aren't worth arguing or getting mad over, learn to just let some stuff go. Don't allow minor people to cause major problems. It's not a crime to take pride in being right, but don't win a dispute and end up losing a friend. Have some tact, some discipline, and some self-control. Think with a royal mindset and know that everybody challenging your throne isn't capable of taking it. Taking your spot won't make them you. The throne is only the throne when the king/queen is sitting there. Otherwise, it's nothing but a peasant in a fancy chair. Pay attention to everything, but don't address everything. If a person feels the need to beg for your attention, it's probably because you've shown them they don't deserve it. Be consistent in that.

Just my thoughts, good people. Just my thoughts.

Not Knowing

Don't complain when something is in your grasp, but you're not able to grab it. Everything that you're supposed to have right now, you have. At times, we can get so caught up in our ideas and what we think we want, we fail to see what it is we really need. It may not make seem "right" , but sometimes God will stop all your progress if you start to lose sight of your purpose. Don't ever overlook the necessity of today. You may not like where you are right now, but you're there for a reason. When God is trying to take something away from you, don't be afraid to let it go. He may be trying to save you some time. When the splendor begins to spoil, don't be too busy to recognize your chance to split. God could be using the "best thing you never had" to bring you to the closer to the "best thing you never knew you needed." Regret looks back, worry looks around, hope looks up, but faith looks within. God will never require you to lose more than he plans to help you gain, but you have to be prepared to receive it all. Inspiration is pointless to a person without motivation. It shouldn't take for everything around you to fall down for you to want to get up. There's a reason for every season, and you have to be prepared to weather the storm regardless of whether you understand its purpose or not. Sometimes not knowing is good, especially when it gets you up and ready to find out.

Just my thoughts, good people. Just my thoughts.

112

The Obvious

Never ignore the things you can't cut off, especially when it comes to your heart, your feelings, and your thoughts. At times emotions can be annoying, but trust that they're there to better you, not to irritate you. Don't use logic to dismiss your gut feelings; allow your intelligence to support your intuition. Avoiding the truth may seem like the safe option, but it's actually the option you choose when you want to meet disappointment. When you have that feeling, you just can't ignore, listen to it. It could be nothing, or it could be the answer to some important unanswered questions. If you don't trust your intuition, you'll never be able to guard your heart properly. Seek the truth only if you're prepared to accept what you find. When you notice yourself ignoring facts just to save a situation, you've just volunteered to get played. When your heart tells you it's time to go, be smart and leave. You can't keep making excuses for people and exceptions for their actions. Some people just don't care. You have to be strong enough to handle the truth, you can't always stop it from hurting you, but you can refuse to let it break you. Use the pain for your progress, the tears for your triumph, and the struggle for your success. Save yourself some time; don't ignore the obvious things; they're right in front of your face for a reason.

Just my thoughts, good people. Just my thoughts.

113

One Way People

Be mindful of those people who feel like your world should revolve around them. The self-serving individuals who have little care for the feelings and consequences of their actions for others. You've got to get out of these one sided relationships. The ones with your jobs, your friends, your family, and your lover. Happiness comes from balance, and we need it in all areas of our lives. If you're allowing a certain area of your life to continuously take without giving, then you're going to unconsciously take without giving from another area of your life. We all want an equal bond that works 50/50, but it's not always likely or possible. On the days when you only have the strength to give 30, you're going to need a partner that's built to give you 70. When you're broken, refuse to be manipulated or led astray, the wrong people will take advantage of you of before they try to fix you. Never allow a person, a job, or anything else to give you less than you would give yourself.

Just my thoughts, good people. Just my thoughts.

Opportunities And Doubt

It's impossible to find new opportunity if you're stuck on the chances you've missed. Look ahead. If your future doesn't seem bright, it's because your attitude is dim. Change the way you look at things. Nothing can stop away-maker, somebody so fixed on the prize that they'll find a way, create away, and if all else fails, pave a way. The only thing that can hinder a focused mind is doubt. When you find yourself using the same excuse for different situations your life is becoming stagnant. Okay, you were hurt - this is a new relationship. Okay, you were fired - this is a new job. Okay, you fell short - this is a new goal. What you try to do says more about you than what you've failed at doing. Nobody can make you great; they can inspire you, maybe even motivate you, but nobody can make it happen for you. Commitment, dedication, sacrifice, faith, and discipline are the five pillars of greatness. At some point, you're going to have to step it up. Excuses won't move your mountains; they just help procrastinate the climb. Those who live life in fear of failure will never meet success. The ones who hide from pain will never be found by love. And the people who refuse to change unconsciously refuse to grow. An open mind opens doors. Don't let your doubt defeat your dreams.

Just my thoughts, good people. Just my thoughts.

Overcome

Small things shouldn't stop you. Small people shouldn't faze you. Small situations shouldn't disturb you. You are on a mission, be focused on getting everything that God has for you. Obstacles are inevitable, but stressing them is optional. Stay focused. True champions embrace challenges because they're addicted to triumph. They don't need or expect everything to be perfect. Sure, they hope for the best of things, but they're prepared for anything. Overcoming is not optional; it's mandatory. Your future depends on it, your success relies on it, and most of all your life deserves it. Smile in the face of adversity because regardless of what comes your way, you know your God didn't build you to break. You are a conqueror. You are a survivor. You are a fighter. You are royalty. You are all this and more. Accept your mistakes, but choose to be greater than your misfortune. The medical definition of crisis is a turning point for better or for worse; it's a moment to decide. So, whatever you're going through, make a decision, be a quitter, or a conqueror. Your decision.

Just my thoughts, good people. Just my thoughts.

Pain Lesson

Whether you care to admit it or not, you've hurt somebody in your lifetime. Regardless of whether it was done intentionally or not, you've done it. We all have, and it doesn't make us any less human, just makes us much more connected. Few realize just how much pain ties us together. We can all identify with loneliness, disappointment, frustration, and anger because we group those experiences together. But none of us will grow, as we should, until we learn the lessons in pain. We have to learn the good in pain and realize that it gives us a different perspective of time. It gives us the time to realize certain things about ourselves. It allows us the time to be smarter, and the time to move forward. It provides us the time to seek wisdom and consider some much needed advice. But perhaps what pain gives us more than anything else, is the strength to be a fighter. We can't ever be so engulfed in our pain that we forget to be understanding, forgiving, and compassionate. You're not the only one who's ever been hurt. Stop being fearless with life, but being a coward with your heart. There are things you'll tolerate and things you will not, but don't blame somebody for crossing the line when you failed to set the boundaries. We base our assumptions for everybody else on our expectations of ourselves. So if you have trust issues, make sure you're the kind of individual who is trustworthy. If you don't articulate how you feel, you're either too hurt to speak or too selfish to talk. And most times it's not because you're too hurt. Pain can either promote you or postpone you. I suggest you learn the good in it, so it can open up the best in you.

Just my thoughts, good people. Just my thoughts.

About Something Real
Rob Hill Sr.

Passion

Only great passions can take your life to great heights. Without passion, there is no true joy, there's no real spark. You may be able to like something, but until you're passionate about it you'll never fully appreciate it. Work hard, but work smart. You can't give your everything to just anything. Be untouchable. Do so in such a way that it cannot be imitated. Most people lose sight of their dreams because things blind them. Be smart enough to know that happiness cannot be found in "stuff". What you have cannot change who you are. Chase your dreams in a way that your nightmares can't keep up. Stress is not a product of true success; stress comes when your desires are placed before what God has told you to do. Money and things can't lead you to your passion; all they can do is give you more distractions to block you from finding it. When you chase a dollar, all you create is another bill. But when you chase a dream, you create a lifestyle. Don't get caught up in the usual route. God's will for you isn't written according to the path that people say you should take. If you want to change your life, get passionate about something. That's the only way true success can ever be reached. Nothing satisfies an ambitious person more than accomplishing a goal. So, no matter how much rain the bad times bring to your parade, begin to use life's challenges as the fuel to a fire within you that cannot be extinguished. Every limitation placed on you should be motivation for you. When you follow your passion, success will follow you.

Just my thoughts, good people. Just my thoughts.

Past Love

The past deserves to stay behind you. Don't hold yourself back wondering about the "what if's" and "could be's". It's pointless. When a door closes, make sure it stays shut. Don't allow people to think they can come in and out of your life when it's convenient for them. You can't let what you left come to where you are. You left it for a reason. Stop wishing things were different. You are where you are for a purpose. Learn to deal with it in a way you can benefit from. Just because the future doesn't look as bright as you dreamed it to be, doesn't mean you give up on your fairytales and settle for your nightmares. You can't always go back to what you're used to. It may be convenient to do, but there's no progress in that. Stop the denial; stop looking for closure; and stop chasing new answers for problems you've already solved. The more anger towards the past you carry in your heart, the less capable you are of loving in the present. What you want isn't always what you get, but if you trust God what you get will be so much better than what you wanted. The past is behind you; learn from it without feeling the need to relive it. Where you're going matters more than what you came from. Meaning, what you do to heal yourself matters much more than who hurt you. This love thing requires a few mistakes before you learn how to get it right and keep it right. Don't become bitter about the past; be better for your future.

Just my thoughts, good people. Just my thoughts.

Patience

If something is really worth it to you, you'll be willing to wait for it. Though people treat patience like it's a past time, it's still a priceless virtue. But these days it seems like patience takes the backseat to convenience. Nobody is willing to wait for anything anymore. If it doesn't come perfect and doesn't come on our time, then we don't want it to come at all. Don't be like most people who are willing to wait on all the wrong things, but are impatient and quit on all the right ones. When you know you deserve things and really feel like something is yours, there's no such thing as it taking too long because you know it's only a matter of time. Patience is the key to endurance. And that key unlocks the door to consistency, which welcomes you in the home of trust. Nothing requires patience like love. Nothing respects patience like trust. And nothing values patience more than happiness. Learn to be patient long enough to let life give you the answers to the questions of your heart. Uncertainty doesn't always mean you're lost; most times uncertainty is just there to remind you to wait on God. Anybody that willingly embraces patience and waits for what they want will never be denied of what they want. A patient man has perfect timing. Just don't use patience as an excuse to procrastinate, patience is divine, but idle time is the Devil's best friend.

Just my thoughts, good people. Just my thoughts.

About Something Real
Rob Hill Sr.

Peace Through Pain

You'll never find peace by trying to avoid life. You can't run from everything you don't understand, and you can't pick and choose what battles will come your way. Being tough is easy because it doesn't require you to be vulnerable. It's easy to make your mouth say you don't care, but not as easy to make your feelings agree. Bitterness and resentment will turn the sweetest of grapes into the driest of raisins. Be careful of the things you allow to change you. Big hearts should never be phased by small hate. Find what works for you. Just because people tell you that something should make you happy, doesn't mean that it actually will. Never try so hard to be a part of something that you start losing parts of yourself. When you settle for "good enough", you'll never get enough of anything worth calling good. Don't let fear trap you when faith is trying to free you. You're not heartless; you're just scared. It's not that you don't believe in love, you're just afraid you'll get it and not know what to do with it. But listen, God didn't intend for you to be hurt forever. Sometimes you have to silence the pain so you can hear the promise. Some breakups are blessings. You may have built a sand castle, but God had to wash it away so he could build you brick house. Refusing to care doesn't secure you peace or protect you from being hurt any more than a seatbelt prevents an accident from happening. You'll find your peace through your pain. You just can't be afraid of the process.

Just my thoughts, good people. Just my thoughts.

People And Simple Things

Life is all about the simple things. It's about the smiles, the laughter, and the joy of living. It's always the simple things that change our lives, and those things never happen when we're looking for them to happen. Most people can't understand simplicity because they're so used to stress, confusion, and uncertainty. When you've been fighting to survive your whole life, it's hard to appreciate peace because all you know is war. But there's value in peace, just as there's virtue in patience. Any fool can get "more" , but wisdom comes from the ability to recognize having enough. When you're able to appreciate the simple things, you're able to enjoy life more because there's less clutter. Be willing to cut the pointless people off. Their irrelevant positions will distract you from your mission. The purpose of making things simple is to get rid of the unnecessary so that the necessary can speak. If all you have around you is people who can't get their life on the right track, it's only a matter of time before they help you get yours off track as well. Of course, you can't turn your back on those who are struggling, but you can't increase somebody else's life if you're barely improving yours. If you're the strongest person in your circle, then your circle is weak. And if you don't have friends that you admire, those friendships should expire. On your down days, you need the kind of people around that you can look up to. 70% of the stress in your life comes from the

124

people in your life. Don't be afraid to be a good friend to yourself and decrease their roles. The greatest step towards a life of simplicity is learning how to let go. Change is the essence of life. Be willing to surrender what you are for what you can become.

Just my thoughts, good people. Just my thoughts.

People Never Get The Flowers While They Can Still Smell Them

RIGHT NOW, today is all you have. Yesterday is forever gone, and tomorrow is but a distant dream. If you aren't letting somebody know you love them at least once a day, then I suggest you start. It doesn't take much to let the people you love and appreciate know just how much they really mean to you. We're all busy, we all have a long list of things to do, but if life hasn't taught you anything, know that there will always be something going on. If it isn't one thing, it's another. Take the time out of your "busy life" and call your loved ones, hear their voices, put pen to paper and write them a love note. Most of the people on their knees every night praying for a better tomorrow, know that they failed to get the best out of whatever blessings God had for them today. Truth is, we don't always get another chance at the quality moments. We find ourselves asking God for once our loved ones have left us. Holding grudges will only hurt you in the end. So the next time you think that sending flowers will replace an apology, put your pride to the side, think again, and let your presence be the roses instead.

Just my thoughts, good people. Just my thoughts.

126

People With Purpose

Throughout the years, you'll lose friends, you'll lose family, and you'll lose lovers. Life journey is a marathon. Yes, everybody begins the race, but few have what it takes to finish it. Stop wasting your time with people who are content with just wasting time. If people aren't adding value to your life, then they need to be subtracted. You need people who contribute to you, who bring you up, and who can increase your situation. Beware of those who claim to care more when their actions show you that they couldn't care less. Some people are around just to be around; don't allow them to take things they can't give. Everybody in your company doesn't deserve to keep your company. Learn to see your presence as a prize that not everybody deserves a chance to win. Great people can't come in if your life if you keep allowing average people to block the door. Sometimes, you just need to remove people from your life. If they don't see your vision, they will compromise your mission. You can't always control whom you lose, but you can control whom you hold on to. Just make sure they're worth it.

Just my thoughts, good people. Just my thoughts.

Perception Is Everything

Whether we agree with it or not, it is. How you portray yourself is the way people will perceive you, and the way you treat yourself is how people will treat you. If you never show people you have a brain, they'll always treat you as if you've lost your mind. However, their opinion of you is never the final authority. Your self-worth can't be validated by others - you are worthy because you say you are. Fools seek approval in things that have no authority, but the wise understand every person passing judgment isn't a judge. You will never be able to control everything spoken about you, but you are responsible for the things you give people to speak on. Yes, your character defines you, but your reputation precedes you. And if you don't care enough to protect it, in one way or another, you'll always be neglected. Secure people are comfortable being hated for who they are; the insecure seek love trying to be something they're not. And at this point in life, if the social you is only doing things in hopes of fitting in, the real you will always end up being left out.

Just my thoughts, good people. Just my thoughts.

Perfect Mistakes

Sometimes, we make mistakes. We hurt people, we lie, and we fail - it's the reality of life. We're human, our intentions are perfect, but our actions will never be. Don't limit yourself just because people place limitations on you. Aspire to be better and strive for excellence because it will motivate you. Don't strive for perfection, as it will only discourage you. Don't be afraid to be criticized, the only way not to be is to do nothing, say nothing, and be nothing, and none of those are options. Greatness is achieved when ordinary people desire to do extraordinary things. Fix your eyes on virtues such as peace of mind, joy, and love. Seek greatness, not perfection, seek happiness, not approval. People will bask in your failures until you show them they've pushed you to your success. A hater is nothing more than a pessimistic admirer. Only a diamond can scratch a diamond, so even when those doubters throw stones still can't faze you. Enjoy your mistakes and embrace your flaws, give up on being perfect and begin working on becoming yourself. Greatness isn't in perfection. It's in originality. And that comes with a few mistakes.

Just my thoughts, good people. Just my thoughts.

Perspective

Sometimes in life you have to step back and look at things from a different angle. In most issues, perspective is everything when it comes to gaining understanding. It's the key factor in determining whether you'll blame yourself for doing wrong or teach yourself a new way to do right. Change the way you look at certain situations, most times when things like relationships fall apart, it's a reflection of your timing, not your inability to love. It's hard to admit that the timing is wrong when you feel like you've been waiting your whole life for something right. It's all about how you look at things. When you find yourself disappointed, it's not always because of your expectations. In most cases, it's your unwillingness to believe that they can be met. The key to your smile is found in your desire for happiness. You don't have to be angry; you don't have to be disappointed, you don't have to be discouraged. You can be as happy as you decide you want to be when you begin to look at things the right way. However, in order to get that smile, you can't be afraid to go through a few situations that may make you frown. Understand this, as long as there is a desire for triumphs, there will be trials. So change your perspective, learn to see the challenges ahead of you as chances to improve you, not as things to deter you. When you really want something, nothing should be able to stop you from getting it. There may be a mountain in your way, but a mountain is nothing to a conqueror. There may be obstacles on your path, but an obstacle is nothing to an over-comer. Stop stressing the fight so much that you forget to claim the victory. God will handle your battles for you when you have the courage to sacrifice for Him. Look up even when the world tells you to look down. The pressure of hard times is necessary to develop and polish fine treasure. Understand that you will make mistakes, but don't beat yourself up about the past. Build yourself up for the future. A simple change of perspective could be the easiest, most effective way toward changing your life.

Just my thoughts, good people. Just my thoughts.

Placing The Blame

You are the way you are because of the choices and decisions you've made for your life. Nobody is responsible for your circumstances but you, and nobody can change your circumstances for you. It doesn't matter if you're 40, if you can't take responsibility for your own actions, you're still a child. Placing the blame on other people to feel better about yourself does nothing to change a situation. That's why hate is so pointless. Accept your mistakes, accept where you came up short, face those facts, handle your fears, and learn from it all. It amazes me how people demand from others what they cannot give themselves. You can't ask for love, if all you do is hate. You can't ask for truth, if all you do is lie. You can't ask for real, if all you are is fake. Ask yourself, is a good person really that hard to find or is it just hard for me to notice one when I see them? It's so easy to place the blame on someone else, but adults take responsibility for themselves. Blaming somebody else for hurting you or breaking your heart will not heal your heart. Stop wasting your time. Accept that what's hurting you now was once everything you wanted. Nobody forced it on you; it was your choice. When you blame others you give up your power to change, be wise enough not do that.

Just my thoughts, good people. Just my thoughts.

Plan With Action

Everybody has an idea, everybody has a dream, everybody has a goal, but not everybody is making progress towards getting them done. What are you doing today to benefit your tomorrow? Choose to be a dreamer with vision, a planner with action, and a goal setter with determination. Don't get so stuck talking about moves that you forget to actually make any. Proper planning is the mark of a mature individual. What you do today will have a profound influence on what you can and cannot do tomorrow. You can become a champion and get over mistakes by being reactive, but to stay a champion you must learn to avoid mistakes by being proactive. It comes down to sacrifice, if your wants come before your needs, you won't meet success until your priorities change. Get ahead to stay ahead. Think first; plan second. Then ACT. There's no better feeling than a good plan coming together. Set your goals, make your plans, and do whatever it is you have to do to make them happen. A plan is only as good as the actions that make it happen.

Just my thoughts, good people. Just my thoughts.

Practice Humility

Some people are more concerned with being admired than they are with being accomplished. They desire to look a part without possessing what it takes to actually play it. What you plan to do should complement the things that you've already completed. Don't get so caught up in your resume that it begins to outshine your actions. People are quick to blast their accomplishments when they're feeling insecure about their failures. However, don't get discouraged when you try and fail. the come up Success isn't supposed to be an easy process. If you're on a journey and the path has no obstacles, it probably doesn't lead anywhere. Never lose sight of the fact that success does not require perfection; it only demands effort. You fall, you get back up. You stumble, you keep on walking. It's not about the mistakes; it's about the mission. Be wise enough to realize that the crowd can't cheer forever. The "hype" will only last until something else happens. Be careful what you do to gain applause that you can't keep. Wait for honor, don't rush for praise, you shouldn't need a round of applause for every accomplishment. In the presence of understanding, explanation is unnecessary. Allow things to stand for themselves. Be secure in what you do. You should never feel the need to have your words justify something your actions display. Average people want to be mentioned; great people want to be remembered. That in itself defines the difference in being congratulated and being celebrated. A lot of people experience moments, but every moment won't create a lifelong memory. When what you're doing is timeless, you're less worried about immediate recognition and more focused on a lasting impression. Modesty is a sign of strength. When you know what you can do and you're confident in it, you won't feel the need to brag about it.

Just my thoughts, good people. Just my thoughts.

Press On

Honestly, I think about giving up at least 4 times a week. I get tired, weary, and fed up. You have those who say stuff like "things could always be worse;" but at times it's hard to find encouragement in that - especially if "worse" is always what happens. At times, life makes it seems like the good people deserve to end up with the hardest times. And it's easy to feel defeated by that fallacy until we realize the answers to our prayers are often waiting for us in the presence of our problems. In a perfect world, when we pray for patience, wisdom, and strength, God would just give it to us. But that's just not how it works. When we pray, what He blesses us with are opportunities to be patient, chances to be wise, and moments to be strong. Life will never give you the triumph without the trials, and when it does, prepare for tribulation. The only way to appreciate being at the top is having a humble understanding of what it took to get there. Though quitting is sometimes a thought in my mind, it's never an option in my life.

Just my thoughts, good people. Just my thoughts.

Problems

90% of every problem in your life is a result of how you act, who you are, and what you do. Don't run from your problems. Running from problems only creates more of them. Whether you want them to or not, your problems will follow you until they are resolved. The root of most frustration comes from the fact that people don't deal with their problems, they just create new situations. And in time, those only birth more problems. You can't move every time your house gets dirty; sooner or later you will have to learn how to clean. Whatever your situation is, deal with it. Avoiding it won't make it better or help it to disappear. Stop using things to take your mind away from what it needs to focus on because it's only wasting your time. When you turn to an activity to avoid an issue, you're stunting your growth. You can't just get around everything. You can't run from every issue, because sooner or later, everything catches up with you. Running from somebody creating problems in your life is pointless until you realize the part of you that attracted them. If you don't address that, the same problem will arise in somebody else. You can change the people in your life a million times, but you'll never have the right people around you if you refuse to change what's inside of you. Fools run from their issues; the wise face them. Be strong enough to deal with things.

Just my thoughts, good people. Just my thoughts.

Progress, Process

You can make something shine, but that doesn't make it treasure. You can buy a trophy, but that won't make you a champion. Fake efforts cannot produce real success. You can fake it hoping to make it, but you'll only be fooling yourself. All progress requires a process. Most people can't get ahead of struggle because they're always trying to get around problems. You have to put in time, work, and dedication to get the things that are really worth having. The things that come fast may be easy to get, but when they leave fast, the regrets aren't as easy to let go. Learn how to take your time. The immature do things fast and wrong; the mature do things slow and right. Patience is the key. Just because you're ready to receive the things you want, doesn't mean what you want is ready for you. Respect the timing of certain things. A good result is the product of a good process. Just make sure you're putting work into places and people that recognize your worth. You can't get a return on your investment if you're investing it into things with no value. If where you're going is really somewhere worth being, the journey will increase your desire to get there, and you won't need a shortcut.

Just my thoughts, good people. Just my thoughts.

Promises And Lies

Your word is all you have. Make sure you keep the promises that you give. Nobody likes to deal with disappointments fueled by false hope, so if you can't keep it real, just keep it to yourself. It's okay to be undecided on certain things. When you don't know, say you don't know. Don't lie and act like you do. If you want your word to have value, it's simple – avoid making promises that you can't keep. Don't avoid expectations; there is nothing wrong with people expecting you to do what you say you're going to do. If being a person of your word is too high of a standard to hold you to, expect your position in my life to be lower than nonexistent. Nobody has time for a liar, but unfortunately, not too many people have the courage to appreciate truth. Honesty, integrity, and trustworthiness aren't just words – they're measures of character. Your value of the truth determines my value of you. If I see you lying to yourself or people you care about, it shows me you'll lie to me. It doesn't matter what it's about. When you're real, the ugly truth is always respected more than a beautiful lie. Don't get so caught up and bound by emotion that you speak words you may not mean and most times can't live up to. If the moment is perfect, just let it be perfect. Don't ruin it with fake I love yous and false hope. Don't promise your heart if somebody else has it. Don't promise your time if you're too busy to give it. Don't make promises period if keeping your word is optional to you. A

139

broken promise is the worst kind of lie. Not only does it disappoint you, but it plays with your emotions. Nobody can make you promise anything, but if you do, stand firm on your word. It's hard to appreciate a person you can't trust, and it's even harder trying to respect a person you can't believe. So, if you can't keep your word, I can't keep you around.

Just my thoughts, good people. Just my thoughts.

Quality Over Quantity

I think we really start living life in the moments where yesterday has no relevance and tomorrow hasn't even crossed our mind. We want whatever moment we're in to last forever. Life probably starts on those days where we don't realize all the things we lack because we know we've been blessed with more than we'll ever need. Yet, I wonder how many people will never be blessed because of their inability to recognize the value of time. Time is the most valuable thing we have besides peace and love. It's one of the few things still on this earth that we can't put a price on. So, we love harder, laugh louder, smile longer, and thank God for the wisdom to appreciate the beauty and the time we've been blessed with today. Wise people know the important thing to cherish is the quality in the moment not the quantity in the time.

Just my thoughts, good people. Just my thoughts.

Quitting

Never quit; the things you're willing to quit on are the things you never really needed or deserved to have. Anybody can start, but few realize that how you finish is all that matters. A great start only has the potential to look good, but a great finish is classic. However, quitters never see the finish to know this. If you choose to quit in anything you start, ultimately, you're quitting on yourself. You have to work for you, to fight for you, and you have to live for you. Don't quit just because you're unsure of how things will turn out. The only way to appreciate the arrival at your destination is knowing what you had to endure to get there. Never start something that you won't be willing to finish. Life is filled with its highs and lows, and the only way to get through them is to find a happy medium. It's natural to think about quitting, but it's stupid to see it as an option. If you see a hurdle on your track to greatness, jump over it, go around it, or knock it over – just don't let it stop you from getting to the finish line. Things may not go exactly as you plan them, but that doesn't mean they aren't happening exactly how God designed them. Detours aren't meant to prevent you from reaching your destination; they just give you another route. Invest yourself in the practice of patience and adopt a mindset of perseverance. Inspiration will get you started, motivation will keep you going, and dedication will help you finish. Never Quit.

Just my thoughts, good people. Just my thoughts.

142

Quitting Versus An Ending

When you stay in sticky situations, you put yourself in a position to get stuck. Don't set yourself up just to get letdown. A person can only break your heart once. After that, you're doing it to yourself. Your mind won't let you stay somewhere your heart shouldn't be, so never ignore your instincts. When the reasons to give up outweigh the reasons to hold on, it's time to let it go. You can't be quick to quit, but you have to be smart enough to realize when the season has changed. Most believe that you should never quit on something you can't go a day without thinking about, however, that doesn't apply to love, people, or relationships. When you know that it's over, it's not called quitting - it's called an ending. Accept that some things come to an end. If the good things lasted forever, you'd never get to enjoy the great. In the process of letting go, understanding is more important than strength. When you understand that something or someone is not good for you, have the wisdom to do what's necessary in letting it go. It won't be easy, but it will be worth it.

Just my thoughts, good people. Just my thoughts.

The Real

Being genuine goes a long way. People appreciate truth, respect honesty, and value sincerity. Be just as authentic as you claim to be, especially when it comes to your word. Don't toy with yourself making excuses for people. Most hearts get broken from lies they've told themselves not from the words of someone else. Recognize the difference between a person with character versus somebody who's just playing a role. Don't make the mistake of taking beauty for quality. Even aluminum foil shines, but it's still not worth much. Know what's for you and what isn't. Everybody that you're real with won't always be real with you. Just because you're a good girl doesn't mean you're the right girl for him. And just because you're a real man doesn't mean you're "the" man for her. Meeting the right person is pointless if the timing is wrong. Be honest with yourself before you hurt yourself. Nobody wants to waste time in a stagnant situation. If you know things aren't going anywhere, be honest, and let the person go. Not knowing how to say something won't stop you from trying to say it. Real will always recognize real. Make sure you're looking familiar.

Just my thoughts, good people. Just my thoughts.

The Real Thing

There is no greater feeling than having something real, having somebody you can trust, and having somebody who believes in you. Despite what most would have you believe, Love isn't some setup, it isn't some trap, and it's not a game. It only seems like that because so many people are playing with it. Games are designed to give you a break from life, not to give you a chance to play with lives. So many couples forget they're fighting for each other because they're too busy fighting everything else. The only relationships that work are the ones that work together. The little things are important, but when you complain about every little thing, it gets harder to see the bigger picture. If you can't be a place of peace for your partner, expect them to retreat to somewhere that is. No man likes to be nagged and no woman wants to be ignored. Find out how to reach each other in a way that brings you closer, not one that creates a divide. The woman that gives a man a chance to relax is the woman who never has to ask for time. The man who gives the woman a reason to smile is the man who never has to ask for loyalty. Find that place of peace; find that person who lets you be you; and once you find that prize, never let it go. Ain't nothing like the real thing.

Just my thoughts, good people. Just my thoughts.

145

Reality Check

If all our days were bliss, then we would never grow. The rough days produce patience, which in turns promotes growth and maturity. Those two qualities are the lead navigators on the road to happiness. The wise understand that sometimes you need a setback in order to set you on the right track. And these days, most minds are so focused on "making moves" that they don't realize that every step forward is not progress. You can take a million steps forward, but if your steps have no direction, you'll never reach your destination. Have a plan and make it plain, because if you don't, you'll be on the road to doing everything but accomplishing nothing.

Just my thoughts, good people. Just my thoughts.

Reasons Not To Quit

In life, we all take losses, but stop looking for excuses and reasons to quit. God promised you the victory, but He didn't say you would go undefeated. Stop waking up ready to throw in the towel – this is not the end. God gave you another chance today because He's waiting for you to begin. Sometimes you're up, sometimes you're down, but the only time you're ever out is when you quit. There's no such thing as being happy all the time. If you lived on Cloud 9, you'd never have anywhere to rise to. Failed relationships, financial hardships, health crises, academic struggles, career delays, family issues – we all go through it, so even when you feel lonely, you're never alone. Whether you know it or not, someone needs you. Somebody is watching you; somebody is praying for you; somebody is depending on you because you are their hope for better days. If you give up, you're robbing the people you are assigned to help of the message of hope that God designed your life to deliver. When you feel broken, keep going. When it hurts, keep loving. When everything in you says stop, go harder. If you quit on your potential, you don't give God the chance to fulfill your purpose. Quitting is not an option, not today, not tomorrow, not ever. When you want to walk out, just think about all the people who were praying for somebody like you to walk in. If your life isn't making a difference, it's because you chose to quit and make an excuse instead.

Just my thoughts, good people. Just my thoughts.

Rejection

Don't ever let the disappointments in life get you afraid to hope. Don't be like most quitters who are more prepared for failure and rejection than they are for success. Refuse to be defined by the times you've fell and embrace them as the lessons that taught you how to fly. Rejection thrives off of fear; be confident enough not to let it bully your potential. When you know you deserve what you're after, it'll take much more than a "no" to stop you. The only dreams that die are the ones you give up and kill. Be wise enough to see that the right "no" can lead you to the perfect "yes." Conquerors don't fear things they can learn from. There is a valuable lesson in everything. Rejection is a necessary step in the pursuit of success. Don't let anything keep you from what you know is for you. If the best you that you can be isn't good enough, you're probably giving it to the wrong thing. All relationships are learning opportunities. Some teach us what we can do better, and some teach us what to never do again. Our negative feelings are choices. Terrible things can happen in life, but you choose how you respond to them. Reject the negative and embrace the positive; it's the best way to change your life.

Just my thoughts, good people. Just my thoughts.

Relationship Talk

Strong relationships are so hard for most people because of the work they represent. Everybody wants everything when it's convenient for them, but things just don't work that way. If it's truly worth having, then it's worth working for. If you really want happiness, you have to step outside of your comfort zone and go get it. Most people fail at relationships because they try to control them rather than enjoy them. A real relationship shouldn't take away from anything that's already in your life; it should add value and compliment all areas. If the one you're in or the one you're yearning for doesn't, stop settling and go get what you deserve. True relationships will require you to grow; they will demand that you change, but that effort should be shared, never one-sided. There's a difference between changing for somebody and changing because of somebody. If they inspire you to change, then it's real, but if you're changing just to appeal to them, it's fake. It's on you to recognize what works for you and what doesn't. You can force the right piece into the wrong puzzle but it will forever be incomplete. Stop wishing things were easier. If it comes easy, it'll leave the same way. Fools fall in lust; the wise work for love.

Just my thoughts, good people. Just my thoughts.

Revoke Your Rights To Rejection

It's sad we let the disappointments in life get us all so afraid to hope. It's like we're more prepared for failure and rejection than we are for success. We're so comfortable in our tendency and ability to fall that we get pissed off at the thought of flying. It just doesn't seem worthy of our dreams or realistic anymore. Rejection is the bully of our potential, and it thrives off fear. However, we should never fear something we can learn from. There is a valuable lesson in everything – even if it's the kind of lesson that hurts to learn. Rejection is nothing more than a necessary step in the pursuit of happiness and success. Don't let anyone, or any rejection, keep you from what you want. Never blame or accuse yourself of not being good enough, especially when you know you're being the best you that you can be. All relationships are learning opportunities, some teach us what we can do better, and some teach us what to never do again. Realize that all our negative feelings are choices. Yes, terrible things can happen in life, but we can choose how we respond to them. Our emotions should never be stronger than our attitude. We'll all deal with rejection, just make sure it's not the kind you digressively accept or inflict on yourself.

Just my thoughts, good people. Just my thoughts.

Saved, Single, Searching

Can somebody give me the real address to love? Because it's not pulling up on my GPS, MapQuest can't recognize it, and Google Maps is tripping. Please God, reveal whoever knows how to get me there because chasing these highs is going to suck if they never protect me from the lows. Why are what I expect and what I get rarely ever on one accord? It's not like I'm asking for much because I don't want that old thing, I'm not searching for that new thing – I'm just praying for that REAL thing. Truth is, no Queen deserves an incomplete King just like no King deserves an unfinished Queen. Get this if you don't get anything else – you don't have to look for a jewel in the junkyard when God promised He'd take you to Tiffany's. Patience is the catalyst to God's blessing; be faithful; walk right; wait on Him.

Just my thoughts, good people. Just my thoughts.

See It Through

Stay focused on your goals. No matter what happens, never lose sight of what you're working to achieve. You don't want to be the person that gets to the finish line, but is still lost because they can't remember why they ran the race. When you feel like giving up, remember what made you hold on for so long in the first place. Times will get hard, but hard times produce patience, which produces endurance. Those two together are the foundations of a conqueror. Sometimes God has to keep blessing you with pain because it's proved to be your most effective teacher. The first step to changing your life starts with your thoughts. The hard way isn't the only way, so put your foolish pride aside, and open up to new things. Bumping your head on the same walls only gets you the same headache. Your ability to adapt to change is vitally connected to the heart of your success. Never lose the vision of where you want to be. If things seem impossible, decrease your doubt and increase your faith. Friends will let you down, family will let you down, and you will let you down. However as conquerors, you learn that sometimes you need to be let down in order to rise up.

Just my thoughts, good people. Just my thoughts.

Selfish Approach

The things you want for yourself have to matter more than what anyone else wants for you. People will have their demands and expectations of you, but you'll never be able to live up to them if you don't meet yours first. It's unfortunate that we can't please everybody, even if we genuinely want to. It's natural to want everything to be "all good;" that's not a crime in itself. The crime is pretending that it is, when you know it really isn't. You may hurt some feelings on the way to your happiness. But don't ever allow somebody to make you feel as if your happiness should come second to their smile. In order for you to care for others, you have to learn the importance in caring for yourself. It's all about how you do things. You can let people know that you come first in your life without making them feel last. Find a healthy balance, some things you can compromise on and some things just shouldn't be compromised. Your happiness will always be one of them. When real love flows, everything else flows with it. In order to respect others time, you have to learn the real value of yours. There's a time to be selfish, and there's a time to be selfless. What good is it to put genuine smiles on those around you if you have to hide behind a fake one?

Just my thoughts, good people. Just my thoughts.

153

Sight, Vision, The Heart

The heart wants what the heart wants. However, we don't always give our hearts the full picture. We only give it things it can cling to. The dreams, the fantasy, the fairytale, but that's not always the truth. Show your heart all the signs you allow your head to ignore. You may see potential in trash, but if the trash only sees itself as trash, it's pointless trying to force it to be treasure. Life is less about what you see and more about what is actually there. Your heart has tunnel vision, once it's set on a sight, that's all it sees. However, your head is there to protect your heart, so don't ignore your instincts. There are so many factors, emotions, and feelings that can have you seeing something that isn't there at all. Gain the gift of vision and the wisdom in discernment. Some have to see things to believe them, but showing me something one time won't make me a believer. Belief requires consistency over time. What you see depends on what you're looking for, so sometimes, you'll have to look past what you feel in order to see what's real. God doesn't give us all the warning signs for no reason. Pay attention past what you see and know more than what you feel. Sight is a blessing, but true vision is divine. You have to show your heart what to see.

Just my thoughts, good people. Just my thoughts.

Slow Risk

Faster isn't always better - learn how to take your time with life. You can't be in a rush to get there first and not know how to last. Focus on what's important, who's important, and what needs to be done. Let go of the rest. Dwelling on the wrong memories may leave your emotions in a maze. Life is a test, and love is a gamble. If you're scared to take risk, you can't complain about the opportunities you'll miss. Some risks have rewards and some have lessons, but what you gain in learning will always outweigh what you lose in ignorance. Don't be fooled; ignorance is not bliss on any level. Chasing the wrong moments can have you losing your forever. Just because you're not with the lover that you want, doesn't mean you're not receiving the love that you need. Decide who's important today and make sure that they know it. Choose what needs to be done right now and be brave enough to make it happen. Always playing catch up is what keeps you behind. Be smart enough to slow things down and get them right while you have the chance. Take love to leave the hate. Take things slow to get them right. Take risk to receive the reward. You win some; you lose some. Either way, you learn that life is a beautiful mystery to be lived, not a problem to be solved.

Just my thoughts, good people. Just my thoughts.

About Something Real
Rob Hill Sr.

Small Goals, Big Dreams

Everyday, I set a goal that I feel can be reached by the end of the day. Nothing spectacular, small goals, like to make 5 people smile or to give 3 strangers a compliment. Some days the goal is simply not to let anybody take my joy or to frustrate me. A wise man once told me that the first step to living big dreams is to start by setting small goals. The second step is refusing to get distracted. The third and final step is to stay in constant prayer. If I've learned nothing in life, I've learned that you can't afford to let anything to take you away from reaching your goals. Life happens. Some days your head will pull you left when your heart is pulling you right, but God will never lead you wrong. When you can't get it right, know that He can't get it wrong. Take it to Him. There will never be a time in your life where some sort of temptation or distraction is not present. Problems don't just go away, and stress just doesn't wear off. As long as you're living, you'll have some kind of challenge to overcome. A person easily distracted is a person easily defeated. The essence of "winning" is having a spirit that refuses to lose. Of course, it's impossible to "win" every single time, but when you refuse to lose, you can never be beaten. True conquerors know that with every defeat, you learn better ways to win. You have to use your setbacks as setups to bounce back. Run from nothing, learn through anything, and pray about everything. Set the small goals that put you closer to living those big dreams.

Just my thoughts, good people. Just my thoughts.

Smiling Faces

If you and somebody always agree, then one of you is lying. Don't let your pride fool you into believing that everybody with an opinion is a hater. The person speaking up probably just cares enough about you to dare you to be better. Respect and cherish those who challenge you in the midst of your crisis. Their eyes may see you as a contestant, but their faith recognizes you as a champion. Watch the company you keep. Every family member isn't familiar and every friend isn't friendly. Jealousy, pessimism, and contentment are diseases passed around more than the common cold. You need people in your life that will constantly challenge you with truth. Don't allow the depressed, misguided, and unmotivated people to hurt you, drag you down, and allow you to lose sight of your direction in life. Misery loves company, and her pity parties always sell out. Cut the dead weight before you become it in other areas of your life. People grow and people change; you have to learn who's worth holding on to and who needs to be let go. Don't just embrace those that say yes and mistake those that say no as doubters. Some people are telling you no because they know you deserve more than what you want. Learn to appreciate those people who will look you in the eyes and tell you that your stuff stinks. They're not doing it to bring you down; they just know that humility is the only way to keep you up. Learn to read through those "smiling faces" and start appreciating your real friends.

Just my thoughts, good people. Just my thoughts.

Sometimes We Need Room To Just....BE

We all need room to grow. We need room to develop, room to learn, and room to make mistakes. Fortunately for some of us, we've been blessed with people around of us who care. They want to help us in our growing and learning processes. They're excited at the potential we hold, and they want to nurture and guide us into the amazing individuals we're destined to be. But sometimes in the midst of their passion, they inadvertently stunt our growth. They don't allow us to spread our wings and fly, as we should. They're so scared we'll try to fly and fail that they keep us under their wing for safety. Sometimes, we have to make them understand that when we're given room for mistakes and failure, we're also given room for growth and success. Maybe it's as cliché as loving somebody and letting them go, but I think the real principle is in loving them enough to let them grow.

Just my thoughts, good people. Just my thoughts.

Spilled Milk

Sometimes in life, we just get stuck. And we're so stuck that we reach the point where we don't know if we even care to be unstuck or not. It's like we're in the driver seat of our own car heading towards our destiny, but for some reason, we have the car in neutral. We don't know whether we want to put it in drive and go forward or put it in reverse and go back. It's like we think we want to run from our past, but don't because it's all we know. And then, we can't run to our future because it has too many uncertainties. All we know is that we're stuck in the now, and we're praying we can press pause on time long enough to ask ourselves redundant questions, flirt with fairytale scenarios, and mentally play out irrelevant options in hopes of figuring out a plan. We think and we think and we think until all we have left is a headache from thoughts we either don't want to be realities or things we don't understand. Nothing wrong with asking questions and seeking answers but we have to know that we'll have three options once the milk spills; clean it up, sit in it, or act like it's not there. No matter what option we choose, whether we choose to cry over the spilled milk or not, the facts show that we'll inevitably have to do what we always do, and that's deal with it.

Just my thoughts, good people. Just my thoughts.

Stay Positive

People fear positivity because it makes them feel inadequate and insecure about not trying. Pessimism and excuses are the foundations of failure. When you fall and get back up going harder than you did before, it baffles people. When you're hurt and you love harder than you ever have, it confuses them because they can't understand what it is in you that they don't have. What it is in you that allows you to keep on going in spite of it all? The best part about an optimist is not that we don't recognize when things are bad; it's understanding we have a choice in making them better. It boils down to attitude; we all get tired and fed up, the only difference amongst us is the fact that some us won't allow that to stop them.

Just my thoughts, good people. Just my thoughts.

Stop The Excuses

Challenge yourself to step outside of your comfort zone. A lot of what you're used to can actually be hindering you. Learn how to compromise; you can't keep leaning on the same excuses for the rest of your life. Sooner or later, you're going to have to find a way around whatever you claim is holding you back. There is nothing wrong with being patient, but you have to recognize when you're just waiting too long. A lot of people are missing out on some amazing things because they are too busy making excuses for why they hold on to the bad stuff. Every relationship problem, every issue on jobs, and every mistake in your life all have one thing in common – YOU. Stop looking for something to blame or hide behind and start being proactive about your life. If you're afraid to mess up, then you're subconsciously afraid to get better. Most people give their all right up until the things they fear, then they start using excuses to justify their lack in effort. When you always come up with a scapegoat expect to meet the wolves. Trying to get around one problem will usually lead you to two more. Solve things, don't make excuses or avoid them. Don't let your excuses block you from seeing what's real. Your opportunities will always leave before your obstacles. Always remember that.

Just my thoughts, good people. Just my thoughts.

Test

Anything that is not tested will fail. People think when they pray for patience, wisdom, and strength that God just gives it to them, but that's not how his will works. When we pray, what he blesses us with are opportunities to be patient, chances to be wise, and moments to be strong. God wants what's best for us, but He requires that we give Him the best of us. He can only get that from testing us and consistently challenging us to be greater. Too many of us are ignoring our blessings and avoiding our miracles because they're all disguised as pain. Dig deeper than what's on the surface. God is never absent, and the only prayers He can't answer are those sent up with doubt. If people are always testing your patience, then that's God increasing your chances at learning to be patient. If your patience is never tested, then how will you know if it's increased? If you're praying for strength, then God is going to send trials your way – He has to give you moments to be strong. Gifts don't always come with a curse, but they will have a price. Don't be the fool who asks for a rainbow, but expects to avoid the rain. If you want God to bless you, be willing to let Him test you.

Just my thoughts, good people. Just my thoughts.

The More You Help, The Less I Try, Because I Know You Got Me

Don't give so much of yourself that when you need you the most, you have nothing left. We're all put into the unique position of being able to help someone at some point in our lives. It's inevitable, and the gift of giving is one of the better pleasures this life has to offer. However, all giving isn't good, and all help isn't beneficial. You'll never really help anyone at all if you're hurting yourself trying to do it. Give what you can, help when and where you can, and allow God to handle the rest. If your loved one falls down, be there to assist them in walking again. Just don't become their permanent crutch. Your desire to see your loved ones grow and fly should always surpass your desire to be needed. And if it doesn't, check yourself.

Just my thoughts, good people. Just my thoughts.

Thank You

Simple words have the biggest meanings. It's amazing the appreciation that can be rendered with a "thank you." Showing gratitude seems to be a lost art these days. That is unfortunate, because there are so many left feeling unappreciated. There aren't too many things that feel worse than giving your all and falling on your face just to be kicked by the very person you were willing to lay it on the line for. Nobody wants to feel forgotten or taken for granted, and nobody deserves to be. We all long to be respected, valued, and cherished in rewarding relationships with our lovers, friends, and family members, and there is no reason why we shouldn't be. So, take the time to thank that person who refuses to give up on you, take the time to thank that person that who goes out their way to make you smile, take the time to thank that person who was smart enough to believe in you when you didn't believe in yourself. Thank that person who always lends their shoulder for you to cry on, or that person who always has the open ear for your problems, or the person that wants nothing but to see you grow. You may feel like you've made it where you are alone, but you owe somebody... a "thank you"... for something. Have the attitude of gratitude. That may seem a cheap concept, but the meaning is priceless.

Just my thoughts, good people. Just my thoughts.

About Something Real
Rob Hill Sr.

The Changes You Don't Recognize

The worst part about trying to change for the better is all the people who'll feel the need to remind you of your past. The ones who'll remind you of all the mistakes you've made and all the times you've come up short. The people who will tell you how important change is to your growth, but ridicule you for doing what it takes to actually grow. I've learned that everybody won't always understand change. They can't comprehend the courage, discipline, and motivation that come with trying to be better. I'm going to mess up, I'm going to fail, and I'm going to fall short, but I'm NOT going to give up. Underachievers in life are the way they are because they're too focused on the fact that they've fell down instead of celebrating the triumphs in getting up. I'm going to try to better every day of my life, and I'm not going to apologize for it. My past does not define me. Though I hold myself accountable for all I've done, I know who I was is not who I am, regardless of who acknowledges it.

Just my thoughts, good people. Just my thoughts.

The Mirror Can Lie, It Doesn't Show You What's Inside.

It's amazing the things a smile can hide. So many people are looking fearless on the outside, but they're haunted by their fears on the inside. What most people don't realize, is that masking how you feel on the surface does not protect you from what you're scared of below it. You can't hide from yourself or your emotions or your disappointments. But you can hide from deliverance, healing, and virtue. Sure, you can try to stay busy, you can try to make new friends, and do new things, but a new thing to an old mindset is pointless. Until you deal with that old pain, your flesh will be living, but your spirit will be dying. Stop thinking you're too real to feel. This isn't a world where you can wear your heart on your sleeve, but that doesn't mean you have to lock your emotions away. When your tears of joy come second to your fear of life, you block your chances of receiving love. Look at yourself, look at your life, look at the people you have around. If you're not pleased with what you see, do something about it. Stop trying to hide behind your job, your organization, or your pride. Gain enough courage to truly be yourself. Until your heart can look in the mirror, what you see in the flesh is a façade. After all, visual proof is the weakest proof of all because deception is aided by perception. Meaning, it's all about what you want to see. The mirror will only reflect what you want to show it, not necessarily who you really are. Don't be afraid to dig deep and find the real you. Not the "you" that the world taught you how to be, but the "you" that you really want to be.

Just my thoughts, good people. Just my thoughts.

Things I've Learned

I've learned to hide behind the jokes and games. I've learned to smile at the right time, laugh at the right time, and escape at the right time. I've learned that too close is uncomfortable and too far is uncontrollable, so I avoid both extremes. I've learned that the possibility of falling in love is probable, but a couple possessing the wisdom and will to know how to stay there is a rarity. Like most people I play it safe. I compromise when convenient, I talk about things on my time, and when I think it's over, I do things including lying to myself just to make sure it stays that way. Then I learned that this is life. The only time playing it safe works is in baseball. I learned you don't get things without taking a chance, and most people in love won't realize how much certain things don't matter until they face the risk of losing it all. I've learned to appreciate love through heartbreak and disappointment. Passion and pleasure never meet their full potential without the presence of pain. Sure, the wounds leave scars. Things never seem to work out on our time, but something else I've learned is that sometimes when things happen slowly, it's a good thing.

Just my thoughts, good people. Just my thoughts.

168

Today > Yesterday

If you have time to sit and mope around about what happened to you, then you're not making anything happen for you. If you're so quick to bring up your past, then it shows that you're not ready for your future. Where you're going will always matter more than where you came from. The love you're giving will always matter more than the love you lost. No matter what you came from, no matter how bad you've been hurt, no matter how hard things get, you can make it through. You just have to want it more than anything. Any pleasure worth having is impossible to get without a little pain. Sometimes, the only way to get your attention is to hurt you. Most people won't change things until they're forced to. Too many people are living through their rearview, and that's what has them continuously crashing in life. Look ahead to the life you want to live. The past is the past. Live in the present and prepare for your future. Stop looking back so much. Stop trying so hard to remember the pain. You're still here because it couldn't break you. You either want to be happy or you don't, make the decision. Once you decide, let it all go and get what's for you. I know some things are easier said than done, but just because it's hard to do, it doesn't mean you can't do it.

Just my thoughts, good people. Just my thoughts.

Too Little; Too Late

Appreciate what you have. I know life gets busy and things come up, but don't lose sight of what's important. Don't take people's presence in your life for granted. When someone has proven that they'll be there for you, value it. The worst mistake is assuming somebody will always be around just because they've been around. There is no worse feeling than realizing you love somebody that used to love you. When you know someone is special to you, never let them feel normal again. Don't say things like "at the end of the day, he/she knows I care," because if you wait until the end of the day, you'll be too late. It's not ironic that we love those who ignore us and ignore those who adore us, it's just plain stupid. When you're being cherished, why waste time trying to get chosen? You shouldn't have to lose something in order to recognize its value. Sure hindsight brings clarity, but if you only learn by losing, there's no way you can ever win. The wise know that foresight preserves happiness; it's easier to keep something right than it is to get it back right. Know what you have before it comes what you had.

Just my thoughts, good people. Just my thoughts.

Too Nice

There is no such thing as being too nice. People can only take advantage of you when you give them the advantage. Be yourself, don't allow people that don't matter to you to change you. When you allow irrelevant people to inspire relevant changes, you're moving backwards. Learn to deal with people on an individual basis. Don't assume that all men/women are the same, just because the men/women you dealt with were similar. When somebody does something to you, handle it with them. Everybody shouldn't have to take on the hell one person created. If people constantly take your kindness for weakness, it's probably because your kindness isn't genuine. People take advantage of fake things because they're disposable, but when something is real, people take care of it, not advantage of it. It's foolish to think you can trust everybody, but it's even more foolish to believe that nobody is trustworthy. Learn to recognize the snakes and be smart enough to realize that everybody isn't one. If you can group all the people in your life into the same category, then you have the wrong people in your life. If you want happiness, get around some happy people. Changing the people around you can really change the things inside you.

Just my thoughts, good people. Just my thoughts.

Toughen Up

You can't always take things personal. Everybody's actions and words shouldn't be altered just to tiptoe around your feelings. Learn how to take the truth for what it is. Assumptions and manipulating words do nothing but create new ways for you to lie to yourself. When you're in a "mood," learn how to check your attitude. People shouldn't have to walk on eggshells just because you're being sensitive. Watch what you say and do when you're mad. Running with feelings can quickly turn to you running from regrets. Anger is a regressive emotion. You don't have to think to be angry, and that's probably why it makes people do and say stupid things. Just because you don't like something doesn't mean everybody doing it is wrong. People should never have to apologize for being themselves. If honesty is what you want and honesty is what you get, complaining should never be a part of what you do. You can't wear your emotions on your sleeve and cry a river when they get hit by the elements. Asking somebody else to change requires you to be prepared to do the same. Be willing to give just as much as you take. It's hard to complain about being hurt if you take everything to heart. Be in tune with your emotions, not ruled by them.

Just my thoughts, good people. Just my thoughts.

Trust

Trust should start off as simple as "I trust you to be who you show me you are." From that point, whether they earn more trust or lose what they started with should be determined by their actions. Everybody won't need to know everything about you as soon as they meet you. Only a fool shows his hand at the beginning of the game. You play things one by one, a card at a time, one date at a time, one conversation at a time. There's no point in rushing something you're unsure about. Realistically, nobody is completely honest with everybody in their life. That doesn't mean lie, but it is wise to hold some things back until they prove they deserve to know. I can't tell you everything about my past if I'm not sure you'll make it to my future. You can't assume you know me; let me show you who I am. Don't base it off what you've heard or what you think you already know. Most of the people who have trust issues don't even realize the issue starts with them. The root of it is based in the fact that most people just don't know how to trust themselves. Nobody remembers your mistakes like you do, and nobody remembers being misled like you do. But realize, when you played the fool, it was you who chose to play. See, the real issue is not that you were lied to; it's that you allowed yourself to believe them. If you're scared to trust because the last time you trusted somebody you got let down, welcome to what we call "life." Realize and accept that you had a part in every disappointment in your life. But let them all go. Your pride can't handle mistakes, but your heart can. I know it's scary when how much you care for a person increases before your level of trust with them does, but don't run. When they show you who they are, believe them, and if they've shown you who they aren't, trust in that.

Just my thoughts, good people. Just my thoughts.

Trust Issues

The things you feel you have to control are the things you don't trust. You may feel secure by dominating situations and manipulating people, but you can't run from the true insecurity that comes with being alone. Everybody has trust issues, but you'll never learn how to trust if you don't give anybody a chance to be trusted. If being hurt is what you're worried about, then you have to get over it and realize you're only hurting yourself. Our thoughts directly influence our actions, so continuously thinking about hurt only creates pain. A closed mind and a cold heart do more damage than any liar ever could. So, stop pushing people away that have proved that they deserve to be in your life. A conditional friendship is a condemned one. If you want to trust, then pay attention to the small details, because in the end, they'll be what made the big differences. Learn through pain; don't run from it. If you never face the challenges, you can never claim the victory. The key to being trusted is simple: make sure your actions align with your words. Consistency earns trust; inconsistency earns doubt. You can either be trusted or you can be doubted, your choice.

Just my thoughts, good people. Just my thoughts.

Trust = Consistency + Time + Repetition

If repetition is the father of learning, then consistency must be the mother of trust. The only things that stay consistent in our lives are the things we trust. Life teaches us to value consistency. It's often overlooked or taken for granted in a world where redundancy or repetition is frowned upon. Nobody likes the same thing over and over, but most of us avoid the risk in change. It's a lose-lose situation; however, while we may under-value the importance of change, we look to those things that change but consistently improve for the better. These are the things we learn to trust. In relationships, we hear the repetition of words but trust the consistency in actions. It's an undeniable bond between the three. If the trust is absent, you're inconsistent in other areas, and if you repeat those inconsistencies all are lost over time. It's a simple formula with monumental proportions.

Just my thoughts, good people. Just my thoughts.

Volunteers And Victims

Know what you're getting yourself into before you get yourself into it. Playing the victim is such an insult to the truth. Man up and be honest with yourself. Many claim to be victims of pain, but most are actually volunteers for it. It's never wise to ignore your conscience. Common sense isn't rare, but the people who actually use it are. Stop looking for a hero. Anybody who really cares about you won't join you in a pity party for pain you could've avoided. Warning signs are there for a reason, don't just ignore them. If the situation starts wrong, it will most likely end wrong. If people show you their hand and you still choose to play, you're no longer the victim but now a volunteer. If your friends are full of drama and you're still claiming them as a friend, you obviously like the drama they're full of. When you walk to a fire expect to feel heat, just be wise enough to stop before you get burned. Don't sign up for disappointment and get mad when you get it. Volunteer for happiness instead of playing victim to whatever is happening. Stop trying to look happy and start actually being happy. Stress is a choice, spite is a decision, and envy is a sickness. Do away these and do better for yourself. You can keep playing the victim or you can start being the victor. It's ultimately up to you.

Just my thoughts, good people. Just my thoughts.

Wasting Time With People

If you are with the wrong person, then you're just with the wrong person. You can love them, adore them, and genuinely want them, but if they're not the one for you, nothing you do will make it work. Unfortunately, people will go through hell trying to save a bad relationship from ending. When it's over, it's over. Sure starting over is hard work, but it beats wasting time. People aren't discouraged about relationships because of the stress they cause, it's more so because they don't know how to recognize when they're wasting their time. Stop thinking you can teach people lessons they don't want to learn. Some people will have the same arguments over and over again just for the sake of looking like they care, not for the purpose of changing. Pay attention to the times where a person's intentions fail to catch up to their actions. Don't fall for that "this is what I'm used to" excuse, because people change when they want to change, and it's as simple as that. Don't mistake a desire to make you happy with a plan to change. Some people are great at pacifying a situation, but horrible at actually fixing the issue. The ability to accept, appreciate, and understand the truth is a priceless virtue. Few people actually know what they want, and that's why so many just take whatever they can get. It's easy to set your standards high on the good days, but when you're discouraged and tired, have what it takes not to settle. You cannot change a person's feelings; it's a waste of time trying to. If the situation starts wrong, it will most likely end wrong. Don't sign up for disappointment and get mad when you get it.

Just my thoughts, good people. Just my thoughts.

Welcome Your Moment

It's foolish to pray that miracles will wait for you in your voicemail; they won't be. Get rid of the doubt in your heart; you have to know that what God has for you is really for you. If you don't, you may over think things and second-guess yourself out of your blessing. Life is short, but it has to be. It's God's way of encouraging you to get focused. He knows that there are a million and a one ways to waste time, and not one way to get any of it back. Be less worried about "why you're here" and concentrate on loving and living the best you can "while you're here." Be courageous, be virtuous, and be passionate about every aspect of your life. It's the only one you've got. Those who are happy with their life know that what you have is worth more than what is missing. When you aren't, you can have the whole world, and it still won't be enough. Truth is, if you never embrace your blessings, God will stop wasting time releasing His favor. Don't just get stuck in the moment. Instead, learn to really live in the moment. Stop being reactive and start being proactive. Welcome your moment and seize all that God has for you. Don't wait until all is lost just to realize it all was there.

Just my thoughts, good people. Just my thoughts.

We're Forgetting To Keep Our Eyes On The Prize

A lot of us are alive, but we're not living. We've gained an "identity" and lost ourselves. We invest our time, energy, and emotions in possessions that will never last beyond the moments we give them. We manage to take care of our belongings better than we do ourselves. We learned to love the money, ignore the evil, and somehow started calling that the good life. What did I miss? When did intangible qualities like humility, integrity and character become irrelevant? When was finding our purpose in life forced to take the backseat to the numbers in our bank accounts, social networks, and other pointless temporary pleasures? It's like we lost the elementary skill to listen and be still in the midst of activity. We all started aggressively making motions toward the "top", but didn't realize we were walking with no sense of direction. We forgot the necessity of patience, the purpose in understanding, and the principles in wisdom. I'm all about living life and maintaining a full and rewarding existence, but maybe when we learn to enjoy the moment we forgot to notice, it was just a small portion of the bigger picture.

Just my thoughts, good people. Just my thoughts.

What About Your Friends

Everything in our lives is in a constant state of change. It's perhaps the most natural part of our growth, and it's expected for us to gain and lose friendships as the purpose for our lives unfold, and we grow. It is very rare that all the people we begin the race in life with actually make it to the finish line with us. Though change and growth are the core reason most friendships fall short, they also fail due to lack of communication, trust, and loyalty issues. With any real friendship, there should be the standard of being real and honest about who we are and what we feel. If we can't trust our friends to do this, we can't ever consistently communicate with them because there can be no real loyalty without trust. Though trust is tough, it's like glass; once it's broken, it's hardly ever the same again. A harsh reality for most of us is the point where we realize that some friendships just don't last forever. Life at its purest form shows us that as people grow, they change. Of course, we'd like to think that all of our closest friends will always be there for us, but most times when things change, people change with them, and they don't always change together. The thing about changes with our friends is the fact that we won't always understand it, and we really aren't always supposed to.

Just my thoughts, good people. Just my thoughts.

What Breaks Hearts?

Disappointment is what breaks hearts. None of that other stuff you hear about. It's the moments where you've expected so much more and received so much less that people are scared of. It's the moments where a face that was once so familiar starts looking more and more like a stranger. It's the moments where that person is all you're thinking about, but their actions show that they're only thinking about themselves. You see, what really breaks hearts is not the flat out lies; it's the half-truths. It's that intuition that has you knowing there's something more to the story that you just can't prove at the moment. Cheaters don't break hearts – it's the disappointers, it's the promises never kept, and the constant excuses. I'd rather have a cheater than a promise breaker. I can handle your flesh being weak, but I can't make excuses for your mind. You see, what really breaks hearts is knowing how great things can be when they're good, and the facing the reality that those moments never last. When you have a good heart in front of you, protect it, cherish it, and don't take it for granted. You'll never be perfect, but people don't want perfect. All they want is effort. In some circumstances you won't be able to do anything about because life happens. But don't break a heart that risked it all just to love you. When you have somebody good, do right by them.

Just my thoughts, good people. Just my thoughts.

What Good Is The Gift Of Sight If You Have No Vision?

We all say the phrase open your eyes. We could be talking about obvious things such as phony friends, being lied to, or blocking our own blessings. Whatever the case may be, a wise person will realize that even though your eyes are open, you mind as well be blind if you have no vision. We set goals, we have our dreams, and we have our plans for the future. We ask God for signs, and we thirst for understanding. But even with open eyes, we lack the vision to see and receive his answers. Know what you're looking at, know what you're looking for, after all even a blind man can open his eyes, but the wise man understands what he sees.

Just my thoughts, good people. Just my thoughts.

What Are You Made Of?

How bad do you really want joy? Is it enough to cut a few people off? How bad do you really want success? Is it enough to lose a little sleep? If people talking about you are able to steal your focus, then you're paying attention to all the wrong things. If people judging or doubting you makes you stop, then you were never really going anywhere. You can't give up, and you can't just stop. There will be some rough days – plenty of them, but you have to persevere. I don't know exactly how you're going to make it through, I don't have all the answers or know all the ways, but it starts with believing that you can. It is God's will that all your needs be supplied. If you knew how important you were, you'd never think twice about giving up. See, you have to refuse to accept that things just have to be the way they've always been. Change is necessary. It doesn't matter whether people want to see you happy or not, you still have to do what you have to do. There are no perfect days, and nothing last forever, but when you're truly appreciating the now, forever is just the icing on the cake. You don't have to play the game because sooner or later, if you stay true to yourself, you'll change the game. Live abundantly now, make history today, do something great. Don't ever allow this fake world to change the real you.

Just my thoughts, good people. Just my thoughts.

What's Good about Pain?

We all dread pain. We protect ourselves in ways so that we will never have to feel it. However, there are key lessons to life learned through pain. I asked a friend what they thought was good about pain, and they gave this answer. "It gives you time. Time to realize certain things about yourself. Time to be stronger. Time to move on. Time to consider somebody's advice. Time to be a fighter. And above all, it gives you time to find yourself and your true happiness." There is good in the worst of anything. Take what you can from any situation, good or bad, and be better from it.

Just my thoughts, good people. Just my thoughts.

What You Ask For

9 out of 10 times, what you get in life is a result of what you ask for. Everything you ask for isn't coming from your mouth either. More than half of it is coming from your attitude and actions. A lot of people complain about the things that come their way, not realizing that they indirectly asked for it. Unhappy people attract haters and drama. Bitter women attract game playing men. Boastful men attract gold digging women. The world gives back to you what you put into it. That's the essence of Karma. It is important for us to be in agreement with ourselves mind, body, and spirit. When your mind wants love and your body wants lusts, there's no way your spirit can prosper. Understand that God has a never-ending desire to bless you, and if those blessings require pain, he will give it to you but for your benefit. If you want a job with more money, you have to be responsible with the funds you're currently receiving. God will give you more when he sees that you're prepared to handle more. He won't give more if you're just going to waste it. A successful relationship with someone else is the fruit of successful efforts to completely love yourself. You can't ask for peace and have an attitude from hell. When your actions are inspired by spite, expect to catch some slight. Don't let what you do block you from what you want. Allow who you are to welcome what you're asking for.

Just my thoughts, good people. Just my thoughts.

When I Live To Love Another Day

When I fall in Love, I'll know it was by choice. I'll know it was because I sought after it or it found me, and I'll know that I chose to receive it. And if by chance my relationship fails, I don't want to be the person that blames Love, I want to take accountability for it. I want to acknowledge those times where I could have compromised but didn't, where I could have given but didn't, and where I should have listened but didn't. I don't want to be the person who forever blames Love for my personal shortcomings. I want to be humble enough to realize that Love is not responsible for those times where I spoke in anger, lashed out in revenge, or blindfolded myself from the truth with fear. I want to be the person who acknowledges their imperfections, but knows Love is still just as perfect as God designed it to be. I want my partner to understand that we complicated things, we ran from chances, and we made mistakes. I want her to know that we loved and learned and didn't fall short just because we loved and lost. I want it to be known that we chose to give pieces of ourselves that were priceless, such as compassion, understanding, and trust. Lastly, I want to have faith that we did what real lovers do when we decided to shine our light and rest assured knowing that nothing can dim the light that shines from within. I want us to know that as long as we breathe, we still live to Love another day.

Just my thoughts, good people. Just my thoughts.

Why Are The Obvious Things We Want In Life, The Hardest Things To Find?

I'm almost certain you will never find anything you're looking for in relationships or love with a closed mind and shut eyes. For most, real love is the greatest thing this life has to offer. It's one of the few things money can't buy and probably the only thing words can't explain. However great love makes you feel, we all know at some point it hurts. We know that once you've found it; it's the hardest thing to keep. But if you expect the greatest thing of your life to be the easiest thing in your life, something is terribly wrong. Nothing is easy; it's not all on the men or all on the women, because none of us can escape pain, yet we all have the same choice once that pain is experienced. Perpetuate the cycle of hurt, or learn from the pain, and create an avenue beneficial to the reconstruction of a clean heart. We all have choices, and sure smooth words work wonders, but a million words of bliss will never replace an act of genuine love. It's amazing what you can see with an open mind and open eyes.

Just my thoughts, good people. Just my thoughts.

Willing To Adapt

Just because you draw it up to go one way in your head doesn't mean that's the plan God has for you. Be willing and able to adapt to change. That's the only way to survive in this world. Humbly accept and embrace change, and it will teach you how to understand failure in ways that will help you open the gates to success. Life will face you with small battles in hopes that you'll gain the tools to keep your heart, eyes, and mind focused on winning the war. The best opportunities rarely come in moments where you're comfortable. They come in the form of your fears and are disguised as work. The size of your sacrifice directly influences the span of your success. When you refuse to adapt, you deny yourself the chance to grow. An open mind opens doors while closed minds complain about being trapped. Be willing to adapt and learn to welcome change. It'll help you find ways to turn the unexpected into opportunity.

Just my thoughts, good people. Just my thoughts.

Word To The Wise

Those who solely give thanks to the food insult the hands that prepared it. On this day, do not only be thankful for all the things that you have, but be thankful for the reasons you have them. Be thankful for all the arguments and tears that cultivated that friendship. Be thankful for those carpooling and bus hopping days while riding in the car on the way to dinner. Be thankful for the moments where you thought you had nothing to be thankful for, because it's in those very moments that we learn just what Thanksgiving is about. It's about those hands you hold around the dinner table. It's about that perfect noise the voices of your family members make. It's about that moment when you stop to close your eyes and realize that even if it's not all good today, you'll still have the faith to thank God in advance anyhow. Key words for today, THANKS and GIVING. It should be a daily practice, but on this day, make a concerted effort to do a lot of both.

Just my thoughts, good people. Just my thoughts.

Working For Pain

How you love is just as important as whom you love. How you got hurt will never be as important as what you do to heal. How you think will always reflect the importance of what you do. Life is cause and effect. It's not always about what happens; it's what you do about it. Pride is trickier than love. It will use your past to make you think you can't handle situations God has already worked out for you. Love doesn't hurt, but relationships can. Know which ones to hold on to and which ones to let go of. Your ability to measure the quality of a person stems directly from your scale of yourself. Protect your heart, but don't neglect your heart. When you avoid love, all you have left to find is pain. There's no need to harbor hurt and resentment. When you've learned from situations, you won't feel the need to hold on to things. Some people are so fascinated with remembering their pain that all they think about are the bad times, the arguments, and the disappointments. Nobody takes responsibility for choosing to stay, for refusing to compromise, or for ignoring the little things. It takes two people for a relationship to come together, and regardless of what your pride tells you, it takes two people for it to fall apart. When love is lost, it doesn't matter who takes the blame, your heart still pays the price. Ask God for a clean heart for He can renew your spirit and increase you. Don't be one of those people who consistently chooses the wrong way. Learn when you're given the chance to. Love isn't hard. People are just difficult.

Just my thoughts, good people. Just my thoughts.

192

You Changing

Never get so fed up or discouraged with life, love, or anything to the point where you stop being you. Life is full of givers and takers. If your circle is full of takers, it's on you to change that. Don't complain about not receiving a return on what you gave, if you gave to people that already showed you they would never give back. It doesn't matter whether its family ties, friendships, or broken relationships - no human bond is ever perfect. However, everything you endure that isn't making you better will ultimately make you worse, IF you let it. Your faith, values, and morals are the root of you. Why let people who weren't even worthy of being with you to change you? Nobody can force you to be anything you don't consent to being. What you allow to change you not only represents you, it defines you. If you let being hurt change you, resentment will soon represent the fear that defines you. So, stop making excuses for who you are. Just because it hurt you doesn't mean it should've changed you. You have to be better than your past. Be the person you are today because that's who you really want to be, not because it's what the past made you think you should be. If you're a lover then love, stop being so scared to "BE" just because of what was. Do you and do you well, just make sure you remain true in the process.

Just my thoughts, good people. Just my thoughts.

Your Changes For The Better Made Me Worse

You can't force a person to be something they don't want to be. Regardless of how much it hurts, we have to face the reality that the vision we have for our family, friends, or lovers just may not coincide with the vision they have for themselves. For most the harshest truth of our love lives is accepting the fact that the one we love isn't the one for us, despite the effort we've put into trying to change and mold them. A good man may not always know how to love, but he will have the desire to. It just takes the right woman with enough patience to teach him. The same for that good woman who may not know how to trust but wants to and waits on that man with the right appreciation for consistency to show her. However, every male won't care to be a King and every woman won't deserve to be a Queen. The fairytales teach you to chase the pauper with potential instead of the prince with purpose because everybody loves to be the exception. You can use a knife as a screwdriver 1000 times over but at the end of the day it's still a knife, not a screwdriver, regardless of how you dress it up. We should pray to change things and leave it to God to change people – especially those we love.

Just my thoughts, good people. Just my thoughts.

From the desk of

Rob Hill

THANK YOU to each and every one of you for taking time out of your busy schedules to read my words. I don't take it for granted one bit. I truly appreciate you all forwarding the "Thoughts for the Day" to your friends, co-workers, and family members. Those of you who write back with comments, compliments, and give both necessary AND welcomed constructive criticism, you all make me better. It makes my day knowing people connect, relate, and are moved by my thoughts.

Sincerely,

Rob

Additional Books by Rob

*I GOT YOU

*FOR SINGLE PEOPLE WHO STILL
UNDERSTAND THE VALUE OF
RELATIONSHIPS

*TRUCE

Website: robhillsr.com

Instagram: robhillsr

Twitter: @RobHillSr

Facebook: RobHillSr